Surprise in Chess

CADOGAN CHESS SERIES

Other titles for the improving player available from Cadogan include:

For a complete catalogue of CADOGAN CHESS books
(which includes the Pergamon Chess and
Maxwell Macmillan Chess lists) please write to:
Cadogan Books plc, 27-29 Berwick Street, London W1V 3RF
Tel: (0171) 287 6555 Fax: (0171) 734 1733

Surprise in Chess

Amatzia Avni

With contributions from Eran Liss, Gad Rechlis,
Ronen Har-Zvi, Artur Kogan, Ilan Manor and Ram Soffer

First published 1998 by Cadogan Books plc, 27-29 Berwick St., London W1V 3RF

Distributed in North America by The Globe Pequot Press, 6 Business Park Rd, P.O. Box 833, Old Saybrook, Connecticut 06475-0833.

British Library Cataloguing in Publication Data
A CIP catalogue record for this book is available from the British Library

ISBN 1 85744 210 5

Edited by Graham Burgess and typeset by Petra Nunn for Gambit Publications Ltd, London

Printed in Great Britain by BPC Wheatons Ltd, Exeter

Contents

Symbols   6
Introduction   7

1   Surprise in Chess   11
2   The Theory of Surprise   16
3   The Five Faces of Surprise in Chess   24
4   Special Cases of Chess Surprise   58
5   More About Surprise in Chess   65
6   The Way Players Experience Surprise   86
7   Summary   101
8   Assorted Surprises   104

Solutions   108
Index of Players and Composers   111

Symbols

+	check
++	double check
#	checkmate
!!	a very strong move; a fantastic move
!	a strong move
!?	an interesting or speculative move, worth trying
?!	a dubious move, for theoretical or practical reasons
?	a bad move; a weak move
??	a horrible move; a blunder
1-0	White wins
½-½	drawn game
0-1	Black wins
Ch	Championship
(n)	nth match game
(56)	see diagram 56 (etc.)

Acknowledgements

Many thanks to **Raaphy Persitz**, whose sharp and focused thinking helped in making the text clearer; to **Eran Liss, Gad Rechlis, Ronen Har-Zvi, Artur Kogan, Ilan Manor** and **Ram Soffer**, for their contributions; and to my wife and children, **Naama, Yuval, Ohad** and **Yael**, for being there.

Amatzia Avni
Ramat-Ilan, Israel
October 1997

Introduction

Twenty years ago, while browsing through an old issue of *Schach Echo*, my eyes rested upon a certain study. I set up the diagrammed position on my board and played over the moves. Somewhere along the line I was startled; the solution contained a brilliant combination, with a rare and unique concept behind it.

The composer of that piece was an Austrian named Helmuth Steniczka. I started to search for more studies by him. His total output was modest, but contained some magnificent works that filled me with elation.

At the time, Steniczka was not regarded as a leading study composer (although in his later years his excellence was internationally recognized). I could not but wonder what had caught my attention in his studies.

1 ♗f5+!

1 ♖b8? ♔xe7 2 ♖xb5 ♖xg6 draws.

1...♔xf5

Or 1...♔f7 2 ♖b8! ♖c5 3 ♖xb5! ♖xb5 4 ♗d7 winning.

2 ♖b8

2 ♖f8+? ♖f6 draws.

2...♖f6!

A smart defence; 2...♖e6 3 ♖xb5+ ♔f6 succumbs to 4 ♖b6! ♔xe7 5 ♖xe6+ ♔xe6 6 ♔e4, etc.

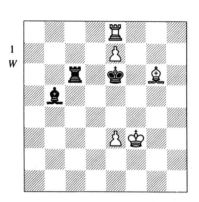

H. Steniczka
Commended, *Schach-Echo*, 1958
White to play and win

3 ♖xb5+ ♔e6+ *(2)*

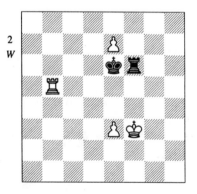

4 ♖f5!!

An astounding point. The rook is captured with check, but meanwhile White improves his king position.

4...♖xf5+

The pawn ending after 4...♔xe7 5 ♖xf6 ♔xf6 6 ♔f4 is also lost.

5 ♔g4 ♔xe7 6 ♔xf5

White wins.

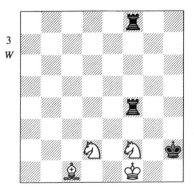

From a study by H. Steniczka, 2nd prize, *Issenger Tourney* 1966
White to play and win

1 ♘e4! ♖xe4 2 ♗a3 ♖ff4 *(4)*

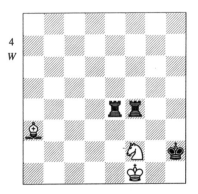

The obvious follow-up seems to be 3 ♗d6, but after 3...♔g3 4 ♗c7

♖c4 White loses. Instead, the big surprise is:

3 ♗c5!! ♔g3

3...♖f6 4 ♗d6+!.

4 ♗d6

A reciprocal zugzwang. Strangely, Black cannot take advantage of the move; quite the contrary in fact!

4...♖d4 5 ♗e5! ♖b4 6 ♔e1 ♖b1+ 7 ♘d1

Draw.

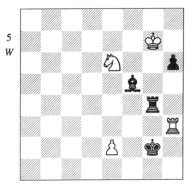

From a study by H. Steniczka, 2nd prize, *2nd Rubinstein Memorial Tourney*, 1972
White to play and draw

The start position appears to be resignable, as White is about to suffer heavy material losses.

1 ♘g5!

What's this?

1...♖xg5+

On 1...hxg5, 2 ♖h5 eliminates Black's last pawn: 2...♔g3 3 ♔f6 ♔f4 4 e3+ with a draw.

2 ♔xh6 ♖g6+ 3 ♔h5 ♔xh3 *(6)*

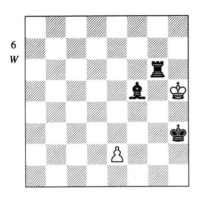

4 e4

White's stalemate idea is clear enough; what is really incredible, is that Black cannot win with a rook and bishop vs pawn.

4...♔g3

Or 4...♖f6 5 ♔g5, again leading a drawn rook vs pawn ending.

5 exf5 ♖a6 6 ♔g5 ♔f3 7 f6 ♔e4 8 f7

With a draw.

See diagram 7.

1 ♔f6 ♖b7!

White was threatening 2 ♖xh7#, and was ready to counter 1...h6 with 2 ♖c5+! dxc5 3 ♖d5#, and 1...♔h6? with 2 ♖cc7.

2 ♖xb7 h6

Now the insidious 3 ♖e7!? (intending 4 ♖c5+!) will be met by 3...♖e1 4 ♖d3 d1♕. A glorious combination now ensues:

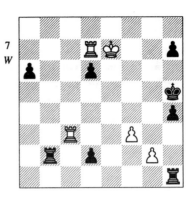

H. Steniczka, 4th prize,
Schach 1991-2
White to play and win

3 ♖d3!! d1♕ *(8)*

4 ♖b1!!

...and White wins.

Black can only choose the mating pattern: 4...♕xb1 5 ♖d5+; 4...♕xf3+ 5 gxf3 ♖xb1 6 ♖d5#; or, the most artistic of all, 4...♕xd3 5 g4+! hxg3 6 ♖xh1#.

To the question 'what is so special', the answer came easily: Steniczka's best works possessed an element of intense **surprise**. The winning or saving moves are not natural, nor obvious, nor in accordance with the logic of the position, nor congruent with preceding play. Rather, they create a sudden shock, an unexpected and unpredictable turn of events.

So, it was the experience of surprise that fascinated me. A question arose: what, in fact, is a chess surprise?

Consulting chess sources provided disappointing, insufficient answers. Comments like 'this move caught me by surprise' or 'when rejecting the draw offer, my opponent was taken by surprise' leave the reader eager to find out why a certain move was so unexpected. What are the characteristics of a surprising move or idea? What is the connection (if such exists) between surprise and other factors? How can surprise be prevented, or dealt with once it occurs?

The sole instance where chess books and periodicals treat 'surprise' in more depth occurs in the opening stage, when a contestant prepares an 'innovation' that forces his opponent off his usual track. Surely, this is too narrow an illustration of 'surprise' in the battle of chess.

Investigating scientific literature, I discovered that 'surprise' is researched in various professional areas: military combat (where it is considered among the basic principles of war), international relations, history, and even psychology (under the headline 'emotions').

The aim of the present book is to outline a chess body of knowledge on the subject of 'surprise'. In doing that, I have been assisted by theories and ideas from the aforementioned fields. Opinions of strong players, whom I consulted, were also of help.

Still, I feel we are on virgin land; there is plenty of research to be done before a well-grounded theory of surprise in chess can be established.

It is my conviction that the insight gained through such work is not only of theoretical interest, but should bear fruit for the industrious student, in the form of tournament points.

1 Surprise in Chess

Chess is widely regarded as the ultimate *logical* game.

Basing their play on certain principles and theorems, players make assumptions, deriving from positional features. They design a plan, taking into account these assumptions and their adversaries' goals. Decisions are made in an objective manner; play is (supposed to be) rational, circumspect, flowing naturally like a river.

In such an ideally pictured chess world, unexpected moves, upheavals and psychological shocks are unheard of. But of course they *do* exist in reality.

The face of *logical* chess is illustrated in the first three examples.

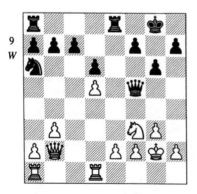

Mikhalchishin – Westerinen
Copenhagen 1979

From the diagram position, White exerts methodical pressure against Black's queenside.

17 b4

Wisely restricting the black knight.

17...♖e4 18 a3 ♖ae8 19 e3 ♖c4

Better seems 19...h5 or 19...g5, in order to seek chances on the other wing.

20 ♖ac1 ♖ee4 21 ♕b3 ♖xc1 22 ♖xc1 ♖e7 23 ♕c4 ♘b8

An attempt to bring the knight back into the game.

24 ♕h4! f6

24...♖d7? 25 ♖xc7!; 24...♕d7? 25 ♘g5 h5 26 ♘e4.

25 ♕d4 b6 26 ♖c4! ♖f7 27 ♕d2 ♔g7 28 e4 ♕d7 29 ♘d4 ♔g8 30 ♕c2 ♕c8 31 ♘e6 ♘a6 32 ♖c6

White pursues his plan slowly but surely. The queen-leaps provoke further weaknesses in the black camp. White's pieces have landed in the holes that were created. The battle is decided.

32...♕e8 33 ♕c4 ♘b8 34 ♖xc7

The harvest begins.

34...♖xc7 35 ♕xc7 ♘d7 36 ♕xd6 ♘e5 37 ♕c7 ♘f7 38 ♕xa7 h5 39 ♕xb6 ♕a4 40 ♕b8+ ♔h7 41 ♕f8 1-0

When first looking through this game, I was impressed (and I still am), by the simplicity and clarity of

White's play. Once the goal had been set, every move fitted the plan.

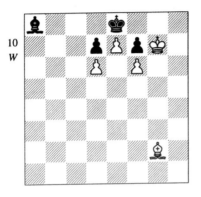

Dr A. Wotawa
Deutsche Schachzeitung, 1956
White to play and win

White's superiority is clear; yet the winning method is very attractive.

1 ♗f1

Avoiding the trap 1 ♗xa8? stalemate, White poses the threat 2 ♗b5.

1...♗c6 2 ♗c4 ♗d5! 3 ♗b5 ♗e6

Since 3...♗c6 4 ♗xc6 loses outright, Black is obliged to choose an inferior post for his bishop.

4 ♗a4 ♗g4 5 ♗b3 ♗h5

4 ♗a4 was a waiting move, forcing Black to give ground. This process is now repeated.

6 ♗a2

6 ♗c4 and 6 ♗d5 are the same.

6...♗g6 7 ♗e6! dxe6

Alternatives are 7...fxe6 8 ♔xg6 and 7...♗h5 8 ♗xd7+.

8 d7+ ♔xd7 9 ♔f8

White wins. A satisfying conclusion, resembling a mathematical puzzle: having systematically arranged the data and determined our options (if x, then y), the right solution readily suggests itself.

Logic prevails not only in positional combats. In many tactical duels too, sacrificial actions spring from solid positional foundations.

Take for instance the next episode, which won a beauty prize in the famous Biel festival. The attack is skilfully handled by White, who overcomes his opponent's stiff defensive efforts. The game impresses with its flow, harmony and aesthetics. But would you say that there is an idea, plan, or even a single move, that can be described as 'unexpected' or 'unnatural'? Hardly.

See diagram 11.

18 ♗g5 ♖d4 19 ♘f6+ ♔g7 20 ♕e3! ♖b4

Not 20...♗xf6? 21 ♗xf6+ ♔xf6 22 ♕xd4+.

21 ♗xc6 bxc6 22 ♖xc6 ♕b8

White wins after 22...♕xc6? 23 ♗h6+! ♔h8 (23...♔xf6?? 24 ♕g5#) 24 ♕xe5.

23 ♗h6+ ♔h8 24 ♖xe6 fxe6 25 ♘d7 ♗d4!

A shrewd defence. However, beyond this or that tactic, Black's king is too exposed to withstand such an onslaught.

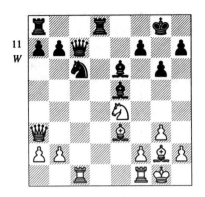

Czerniak – Richi
Biel 1981

26 ♕xe6 ♕e8 27 ♕d6 ♕e4 28 ♘f6! ♕b7 29 a3 ♖c4 30 b3 ♕c6

Black continues to find 'only' moves. Alas, the position just cannot be maintained. White's next cuts short the agony.

31 ♗g7+! ♔xg7 32 ♕e7+ ♔h6 33 ♘g4+ 1-0

This form of 'exemplary chess' (logical, sensible, comprehensible, flowing) is the one advocated in instruction manuals. But frequently the chess we know and play assumes a different form.

Bertok – Damjanović
Yugoslavia 1966
Réti Opening

1 ♘f3 d5 2 g3 c6 3 ♗g2 ♗g4 4 d3 ♗xf3 5 exf3 ♘f6 6 0-0 e6 7 ♘d2 ♗e7 8 f4 0-0 9 ♘f3 c5!? 10 ♘e5

♘c6!? 11 ♘xc6 bxc6 12 c4! ♖b8 13 ♖e1 ♖e8 14 ♕a4!? ♗f8 15 b3 ♕c8 16 ♗b2 ♖d8 17 f5 exf5 18 ♗xf6 gxf6 19 ♗h3! dxc4 20 dxc4 ♖d2 21 ♖e3 ♕d7 *(12)*

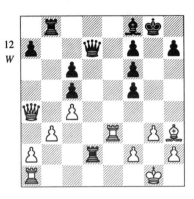

Black's pawn formation makes us shudder. It seems that White has a definite edge. He now relaxes and makes a waiting move. The intensity and speed of the counter-offensive that follows are amazing.

22 ♔g2??

Correct was 22 ♖ae1, followed by 23 ♖f3, but Black would have reasonable chances even in this case. Appearances notwithstanding, the diagram position is not that bad for him.

22...♕d4! 23 ♖ae1

Forced, as *both* white rooks were threatened.

23...♖e8! 24 ♔g1 f4 25 gxf4 ♕xf4 26 ♖g3+ ♔h8 27 ♖f1 ♖e1! 0-1

28 ♖g2 ♖xf1+ 29 ♔xf1 ♕f3 is curtains. The swift transformation

that took place in the last few moves is bewildering.

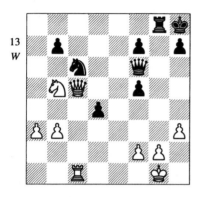

13
W

Deep Blue – Kasparov
Philadelphia match (1) 1996

Shortly before the diagram position arose, the world champion made clear his aggressive intentions by playing ...♔g8-h8 and ...♖c8-g8. Surprisingly, the machine nonchalantly carries on with its queenside play:

28 ♘d6 f4 29 ♘xb7!

White grabs a distant pawn and disregards his king's defence. Yet it is the right approach.

29...♘e5 30 ♕d5 f3 31 g3 ♘d3

31...♕f4, with the double threat 32...♕xc1+ and 32...♖xg3+, is met by 32 ♖c8!.

32 ♖c7 ♖e8

Black's initiative assumes frightening dimensions.

33 ♘d6! ♖e1+ 34 ♔h2 ♘xf2

Now White's king seems doomed.

However, the computer has everything under control.

35 ♘xf7+ ♔g7

If 35...♕xf7, then 36 ♕d8+! ♖e8 (36...♕e8?/♕g8? 37 ♕f6+) 37 ♕xd4+ ♔g8 38 ♖xf7 ♔xf7 39 ♕d5+ (also 39 ♕xf2 ♖e2 40 ♔g1) 39...♔ any 40 ♕xf3 and White wins.

36 ♘g5+ ♔h6 37 ♖xh7+ 1-0

He does not bother to wait for 37...♔g6 38 ♕g8+ ♔f5 39 ♘xf3.

A sensational game. Deep Blue's performance (impertinently ignoring the enemy's threats, and indulging itself in pawn-snatching) was totally unexpected.

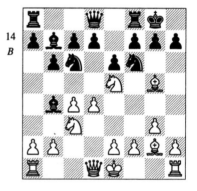

14
B

Plaskett – Speelman
London Lloyds Bank 1993

There are times when a single move leaves us shaking our heads with astonishment:

8...♘xe5

The apparently pinned knight suddenly moves: Black is ready to invest an exchange for a pawn and a good position: 9 ♗xb7 ♘xc4 10 ♗xa8 ♕xa8. White tries to interpolate the exchange...

9 ♗xf6

...to be stunned by...

9...♕c8!!

How can this work? The variations are simple (10 ♗xe5 ♗xg2 or 10 ♗xb7 ♕xb7) but in this particular case the concept of non-capture is strikingly original.

10 ♗xe5 ♗xg2 11 ♖g1 ♗xc3+ 12 bxc3 ♗b7 13 c5?! d6! 14 cxd6 cxd6 15 ♗xd6 ♖d8 with the better game for Black (0-1, 25).

And then, sometimes the whole set-up of one side generates an illogical impression:

Gelfand – Shirov
Linares 1993
Réti Opening

1 c4 e6 2 ♘f3 d5 3 g3 c6 4 b3 a5 5 ♗b2 a4 6 ♗g2 a3!? 7 ♗c3 b5?!

Hasn't the Latvian star heard of piece development?

8 c5 ♘f6 9 b4 ♘e4 10 0-0?! ♘xc3 11 ♘xc3?!

Successive inaccuracies. On his tenth move, 10 ♕b3 was superior; on his last move, 11 dxc3 was better.

11...d4! 12 ♘e4 f5 13 ♘eg5 *(15)*

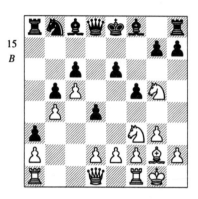

Total underdevelopment of the black army. Yet, although Black has played the opening 'against the rules', his position is now at least equal! (0-1, 39).

The last four examples provide abundant proof that chess is not always as logical, coherent and ordered as we might like to think. Many games comprise turns, discontinuity, even reversals. From here on, we shall focus our attention on the unexpected, *surprising* side of chess.

2 The Theory of Surprise: Abstract

Definition

Surprise is defined in the dictionary as something unexpected, sudden, which occurs without warning.

Broader definitions in the military context are, for example:

"(Surprise takes place) to the degree that the victim does not appreciate whether, when, where or how the adversary will strike" (Betts, 1982).

"An attack launched against an opponent who is insufficiently prepared in relation to his potential resources" (Brodin, 1978).

It follows that the basic ingredient of surprise, is that *it occurs contrary to the enemy's expectations*; and *catches him unwary and unready.*

Various approaches

Being a complex, multi-dimensional phenomenon, attempts have been made to dissect surprise into components, exploring it from the *victim's* angle, as well as from the *initiator's* point of view; or analysing it as a function of *its intensity* (on a scale from no surprise to total surprise).

Other types of classification are of *surprise attack* vs *defensive* (a pre-emptive, first-strike operation) *surprise*; of *tactical* vs *strategic surprise*.

The phenomenon may be looked at as an *emotional state*; a *physiological* state; a *personal* vs *organizational* event... In short, behind this simple word 'surprise' lurks a variety of meanings and interpretations.

The importance of surprise

Surprise is sought because it reduces the costs of facing a fully prepared adversary. Experience teaches that the ratio between the effort expended in initiating a surprise and the results obtained with it favours the initiator.

Surprise is considered as a **force-multiplier**; it does not merely enhance the value of strong moves or plans; it multiplies their effect.

In military action, the very possibility of surprising the enemy is a significant consideration in deciding whether and when to declare war.

The impact of surprise

Why is surprise so strong a weapon? Because it has a devastating impact on an unprepared opponent.

Surprise "confuses the enemy and lowers his morale" (Clausewitz).

It "throws an enemy off-balance and causes him to react rather than dictate terms of battle" (Oddell, 1992).

When surprised, one's ongoing activity is momentarily halted. "The mind seems to be blank... It is a little like receiving a mild electric shock... You do not know exactly how to react. There is a feeling of uncertainty" (Izard, 1991).

True, surprise alone does not assure ultimate victory; it is a transient state that comes and goes quickly. If the surprised party survives its consequences, he may fight on with success, and even turn the tables.

Principles of surprise

Military theoreticians of the former Soviet army treated surprise as an evasive concept, difficult to categorize. "It is impossible to recommend ... permanent methods of achieving surprise ... Its forms, methods and techniques ... are altered ... depending upon specific circumstances" (Kirian, 1986).

While no two strategies of surprise are exactly alike, all surprises seem to be guided by a limited set of principles. Successful surprise requires the surpriser to:

- **Penetrate the opponent's mind,** understanding what his expectations are.
- **Conceive a high-quality idea** that frustrates these expectations.
- **Support the idea with solid data and deep analysis** of the situation.
- **Plan carefully** the execution of surprise.
- **Manipulate the enemy's sense of vulnerability,** so that he will feel secure.
- **Camouflage one's intentions** (naturally, otherwise the effect of surprise is diminished).
- **Execute the surprise speedily.** Quickness deprives the enemy of sufficient time to organize an adequate defence.
- **Use surprise only when it is essential** (e.g. there is no point in taking risks in a winning position).

Psychological factors that make surprise feasible

Based on historical analysis, researchers conclude that surprise attacks have a very good chance of succeeding. Experts, headed by Twining (1992), emphasize two predominant variables that account for a victim's receptivity to his enemy's planned surprise. These are **perception and cognition**.

On the perceptual level, there are certain biases that influence receptivity to new data:

- People tend to ignore information that does not fit the frame of their preconceptions.
- Alternatively, they distort that information, to make it comply with their expectations. They assimilate ambiguous data in a way that reaffirms their established views.
- They find it difficult to distinguish a vital piece of data from a vast amount of information (to decompose 'signal' from 'noise', in another terminology).

On the cognitive level, there are certain biases of the human brain that affect the processing of information in irrational ways:

- A tendency to project attributes in one area to other spheres (e.g. concluding, on the basis of a poor attacking operation, that the opponent is weak also in his defensive ability).
- A tendency to cling to former views, in order to appear consistent.
- A tendency to recall vividly frequent events, or events that stand out.
- A tendency to be more confident than is warranted by facts, especially in

difficult, complex, uncertain situations.

- A tendency to project one's own preconceptions, beliefs and rationale to the enemy, assuming he will look at things the way we do.
- A tendency to assume that the future will be an extrapolation of the past, e.g. that the enemy will continue to act as he had done previously.

Among other factors that may lead us astray when trying to predict an impending surprise are:

- A limited imagination (which cannot fathom what lies in store).
- An inherent difficulty to understand one's opponent's character, his motives, his willingness to take risks...
- A shortage of data regarding the enemy's strength, the weapons in his possession, etc.

So, we receive and absorb information in far from objective, rational ways.

This, naturally, creates blind spots that make us prone to surprise attacks. Fortunately, the same biases apply to our adversaries, thus assisting us to spring our own surprises!

The faces of surprise

Surprise may appear in many forms. That is one reason why it is difficult to forestall. One can realize the exact location where the enemy will strike, and still be caught unprepared as to the timing of his attack, or to the type of weapons he will be using. A customary classification of various surprises is presented below:

Surprise in intention

Causing our opponent to misjudge our ambitions; making him believe that our aim is peace, when in reality it is war; or vice versa.

Surprise in location

Choosing unexpected points for attack, or conducting a battle on unexpected terrain.

Surprise in time

Timing our attack at an unlikely moment (considering the enemy's expectations). 'Unlikely' can be, for example, at a very early stage, before the troops are well organized; or too late, e.g. when the forces are there, but we still continue to manoeuvre.

Surprise in doctrine

Changing our ordinary conduct of battle; devising new ways of deploying one's forces, a different outlook on the concept of deterrence, etc.

Surprise in technology

Using innovative types of weapons; implementing novel forms of logistics, transportation, etc.

The many facets of surprise reflect its multidimensionality. Each side in a war asks himself:

- *What* will the enemy do? (intention)
- *Where* will he attempt a breakthrough? (location)
- *When* will he attack? (time)
- *How* does he plan to do it? (doctrine)
- *With what* means does he intend to carry out his plans? (technology)

Surprise can take any of these forms. It can also appear as a combination of several aspects. This is not incidental – since a chain-reaction is likely to ensue: "Erroneous assumptions about whether the attack will occur, must lead to erroneous expectations with regard to its timing; and sometimes, to its location and the way it is carried out" (Kam, 1988).

Related variables

Deception and surprise

Deception, defined as "measures intended to fabricate, confuse, distort or deny information that could be of value (to the enemy)" (in Hybel, 1986), is an important contribution to achieving surprise. Means of deception include **masking** (concealing what is done) and **misleading** (creating a false impression, suggesting to the enemy that something else is done).

Techniques such as disinformation and transmitting calming messages are used. It is agreed that the number of stratagems used to achieve surprise is quite small.

Risk and surprise

Planning a surprise usually involves a certain degree of risk. Our adversary may be fully prepared, or the idea underlying the surprise may turn sour.

Researchers have noted that risk evaluation is totally subjective. What appears to one side crazy and irrational, may seem viable to the other. As Betts (1982) correctly points out, when weighing the pros and cons of alternative ways of action, the cost of the 'risky' way should be compared to the cost of not taking any risk (which is sometimes greater).

Deterrence and surprise

As a rule, the stronger one's position, the less one is afraid of being surprised; one tends to believe that if the enemy has some sense left, he will not dare to attack, bearing the consequences.

Paradoxically, exactly this line of reasoning tempts the weaker side to deliver a surprise attack. The chances of it being a **real surprise** are very good! (Handel, 1976). Hence, the chances of a powerful army with awesome weapons being surprised, are ambiguous.

Warning signals and surprise

Successful surprise depends, by definition, on the failure of the enemy's warning systems. Such failure can stem from lack of information; when one is ignorant of the enemy's intentions. It can also take place when information exists, but is wrongly evaluated.

Hence, knowledge of the enemy's plans is a **necessary** condition for avoiding surprise, but is **insufficient** in itself. Understanding one's rival's general strategy does not mean that a particular action will be anticipated.

Confronting surprise

Preventive measures

How can surprise be avoided? The common-sense approach would be to adopt an ever-alert, suspicious state of mind. But as Betts (1982) mentions, slogans as 'anything can happen' or 'be ready for everything' may be good in principle, but not very helpful in practice. It is hardly possible to prepare and devise counter-measures against *every* conceivable threat.

Understanding the logic and patterns of surprise does not guarantee that a sudden attack shall be repulsed. "Its repeatedness and the cognition that it will arrive, does not make us less vulnerable to its impact" (Kam, 1988).

Is prevention possible, then? Twining (1992) states that behavioural experiments, empirical data and historical case-studies point at the inherent difficulty of preventing surprise. "In most cases, it simply cannot be done" – he concludes, pessimistically.

Others, like Hybel (1986), believe that understanding the phenomenon of surprise can minimize its occurrence.

It seems that at least *some* preventive methods can reduce the probability of future surprise.

One is **awareness**: assimilating the cognition that an opponent may always have a surprise in store for us. As long ago as 1944, the Soviet army's 'regulations' included a paragraph stating that the enemy will seek to spring a surprise, and that a high degree of vigilance, preparedness and security must be kept.

Second, there is **training and specializing**: exercising and raising one's professional skills should help decrease the number of situations, plans and tactical operations that will come as a surprise.

Third, is **building hypothetical scenarios** of what the enemy might do [in chess terms, that means trying to guess the choice of his opening; his ambitions for the game (ranging from 'winning at all costs' to 'losing with dignity'); anticipating the way the game will evolve (tactical/positional, closed/open...)] and preparing specific courses of action against various options.

Fourth, is developing a **warning system**: signals that will assist in identifying an approaching danger.

Fifth, there is **deterrence**: leading one's opponent to believe that if he tries to catch us by surprise, he will pay dearly.

Finally, there is the option of **striking one's own surprise first** (pre-emptive defensive measures), forcing one's adversary to diverge from his intended plans, before he unleashes his prepared surprise.

This first blow may be goaded by fear rather than bravery.

Countering measures

Researchers from non-chessic worlds do not lay much store on preventive methods. They see more promise in devising plans and strategies designed to deal with surprise, once it occurs, thereby minimizing its effects.

Oddell (1992) suggests planning a force-structure that will survive a surprise attack, and rebound quickly with counterattack, manoeuvre and initiative.

Another recommendation, psychologically oriented, is to develop a measure of toughness: not getting too excited or upset when encountering a surprising manoeuvre or an unforeseen tactical step.

This advice is geared towards fending off the impact of surprise by **intrapersonal** means.

An essential trait in combating surprise is *flexibility*. He who sticks blindly to his master-plan may be destroyed by surprise, since he has not left options open for himself. He who is ready to switch plans to suit changed circumstances, will have better chances to survive.

Conclusion

We have presented a summary of current knowledge on surprise, embedded in military context[1]. It should be viewed as a guide, but we had better remember that the analogy between chess and war is not perfect.

In real life, hostility breaks out from a state of peace; in chess, it is a war from the first move. The game commences from an equal position (well, OK, White is a little better); a real war does not. In chess each player sees the whole 'battlefield' in real time; no piece of data escapes him. In war, even in this technological, fast-communicating age, the commanding general has to rely on secondary sources in order to grasp the whole picture. Chess players move alternately, one move at a time; the antagonists in war can make several moves in succession.

Another important difference is that the will to take risks in real war, where people's lives and political careers are at stake, is not quite the same as in a chess battle.

Therefore, our mission from now on will be to take a close look at the phenomenon of surprise **in the context of the royal game**, trying to produce valuable and relevant insights.

Bibliography

1. *Surprise Attack* / R. K. Betts / The Brookings Institution / USA, 1982

---

1   Amongst interesting applications of surprise in other domains, we would mention i*t*s use in devising *critical interventions in psychotherapy*, that give a new direction to treatment, or to a patient's life (Omer, 1994); and the rules that determine demarcation *of boundaries* in which surprise can take place, in the theory of play (Rapp, 1984).

2. *Strategic Surprise in the Age of Glasnost* / D. T. Twining / Transaction Publishers / USA, 1992

3. *The Logic of Surprise in International Conflict* / A. R. Hybel / Lexington Books, 1986

4. *Surprise Attack* / E. Kam / Harvard University Press, 1988

5. *Surprise: The Korean Case-Study* / P. Oddell / Naval War College, Newport, USA, 1992

6. *Principles of War* / from *War and Strategy* / Y. Harchaby / 1980 (in Hebrew)

7. *Surprise: Getting the Enemy Off-Balance* / G. Rotem (ed.) / IDF, 1992 (in Hebrew)

8. *Surprise in Offensive Operations of the Great Patriotic War* / M. M. Kirian / Science Publishing House / Moscow, 1986 (in Russian)

9. *The Psychology of Emotions* / C. E. Izard / Plenum Press, 1991

10. *Aspects of Consciousness and Personality in Terms of Differential Emotions Theory* / C. E. Izard and S. Buechler / from *Emotions: Theory, Research and Experience, Vol. 1* / R.Plutchik and H. Kellerman (eds.) / Academic Press, 1980

11. *Encyclopedia of Psychology* / R. J. Consini (ed.) / 2nd ed., Vol. 3 / John Wiley and Sons, 1994

12. *Clausewitz, on War* / M. Howard and P. Paret (eds.) / Princeton University Press, 1976

13. *Surprise Attack: The Case of Sweden* / K. Brodin / Journal of Strategic Studies, Vol. 1 / 1978

14. *Perception, Deception and Surprise* / M. Handle / Jerusalem, 1976

15. *Critical Interventions in Psychotherapy* / H. Omer / Norton, 1994

16. *The World of Play* / U. Rapp / IDF Publishing House, Israel, 1984 (in Hebrew)

3 The Five Faces of Surprise in Chess

Psychologists regard surprise as having no *a priori* valence. It cannot be classified as 'good' or 'bad'. Only past experience will crystallize one's attitude to future surprises.

Yet in the specific context of the game of chess, where a competent player is required to see some moves ahead, surprise is definitely a loaded concept: to be surprised is, in most cases, a negative event[1].

As a testimony of that, we need only consider that it is a chess player's occupational nightmare to be caught in the opening by a new, carefully planned move, that alters the assessment of a position[2].

Do you recall the definition of surprise? Its main characteristic was **unexpectedness**. Therefore it seems a good idea to clarify to ourselves what is expected in chess: what does a player expect his opponent to do?

If we can understand this, we shall gain a better insight into what constitutes a surprise in chess, i.e. a sharp deviation from, or even a reversal of, expected behaviour.

Let us now review the five faces of surprise, introduced in the preceding chapter.

A. Surprise in intention

The game begins. Our opponent makes a move and starts the clock. We wonder: What are his ambitions? Will he try for a win, or be satisfied with a draw? And perhaps, when there are large differences in rating, has the enemy mentally reconciled himself to eventual defeat, and is only seeking to exhibit prolonged resistance, putting up a hard fight?

Suppose the adversary strives for victory. Is everything clear now? Not quite. Some questions remain: *how much* does he want to win, and *how far* will he strain to attain it?

After his return match against Botvinnik in 1961, in which he lost

---

1   Even when the opponent falters and we are pleasantly surprised, the immediate, reflective emotion is negative.

2   In this respect, chess players are like managers; their fear of being surprised is reflected in their desire to be in total control, at all times, in all places.

his title, Mikhail Tal was asked what he thought was the main reason for his defeat. The ex-world champion answered swiftly: "Botvinnik's determination! I never could have imagined that he could be so resolute in play!" (Vasiliev, 1975).

A1) Expected behaviour: **The enemy's efforts to win are dependent upon the rewards he stands to gain.**

A player will try hard for victory, if it will assist him in attaining a coveted goal: overall victory in the tournament, a money prize, qualifying to the next stage, or fulfilling the requirements to a higher grade. Even the inner satisfaction derived from an original idea or combination will raise his motivation.

Possible surprises:

A1.1) Some players (Bobby Fischer was a notable example) *always* play to win, regardless of incentives.

A1.2) Motivation level can rise during play, if one feels challenged:
"At the 1955 Interzonal in Gothenburg, Ilivitsky's game against Guimard was adjourned ... Ilivitsky decided to try to win, in view of all the misfortunes which had pursued Guimard in the previous rounds and his apparent indifference, as if he

had given up the tournament ... (During resumption) the Argentinean drearily, seemingly without a spark of interest, stared at the position. My impression was that ... he was dozing. Ilivitsky chose an active and very committal move. Guimard roused himself. He changed beyond recognition, his eyes became decisive ... he began an attack ... it was obvious that he was thirsting for battle. [he won]" (Krogius, 1976).

A1.3) Some players are so cautious that they will not play for a win in an equal position, even when victory is vital for them.

A2) Expected behaviour: **A player's ambitions in a game are greatly affected by his assessment of the position and by the strength of his opponent.**

Victory cannot be attained by miracles. If one's position is objectively worse, and one's opponent strong, there is no sense in playing for a win: a draw is the most one can realistically hope for.

Possible surprises:

If a player ignores objective considerations, and his aims are to head for victory at all costs, then his opponent is likely to be surprised! He might have doubts, may become anxious... Alternatively he may get irritated, upset, or even feel offended.

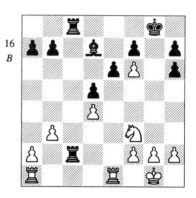

A3) Expected behaviour: **A player who offers a draw is peacefully inclined**.

The assumption appears tautological: he who offers a draw wants to split the point – right?

Possible surprises:

Much has been said and written on the topic of draw offers. In a controversial and thought-provoking article, GM Fishbein (1993) looks at draw offers as psychological ploys. He goes as far as to suggest that "sometimes, when playing for a win, offering a draw is the best move you can make" (!). His rationale is that stirred by the offer of a draw, one's opponent tends to become overconfident and starts playing for a win.

Here is one of his examples (see diagram 16):

The f6-pawn seems to give White an advantage in the ensuing middle-game. However...

22...♗b5! 23 ♘e5 ♗e2!

...prevents White from activating his rooks.

24 f3 ♖8c3!

Here Black offered a draw. Objectively, White had no reason to decline.

Fishbein – D. Root
American Open 1990

**25 ♘g4 h5! 26 ♘f2 h6! 27 ♘h3?
♗xf3! 28 gxf3 ♖xf3**

The white knight is trapped.

29 ♖ac1 ♖xc1

But not 29...♖xa2? 30 ♔h1! ♖xh3 31 ♖g1+ when White wins.

30 ♖xc1 ♖xh3

...and Black eventually won.

"It is highly doubtful that I would have invented the manoeuvre ♘g4-f2-h3, had not [my opponent] offered a draw" (Fishbein).

Here is another example (see diagram 17). White, in a strategically inferior position, has just captured a black knight on d5 (**16 ♘xd5**) and offered a draw.

Anand's refusal was certain, dictated by the match score. So, why the offer?

"Kasparov claimed after the game that he had never expected Anand

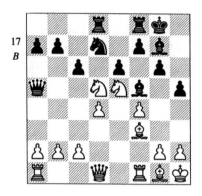

Kasparov – Anand
New York World Ch match (14) 1995

to accept the draw offer, but he was using it to probe Anand, and see how confident he was at that moment. (Since Anand pondered before declining the offer, Kasparov) could tell that Anand was not sure of himself..." (Wolff, 1995).

A4) Expected behaviour: **Given what he needs (win or draw), a player will settle for it**.

Possible surprises:

In 1984, I witnessed a strange incident: two masters were paired in the final round of the semi-finals of the Israeli championship. Both needed half a point to qualify. A victory didn't matter; a loss was insufficient. There were no additional incentives (such as money prizes) for either player.

After about 8-10 ordinary moves, White offered a draw. Black deliberated and decided to reject the offer. White was stunned by the refusal and lost without resistance.

In conclusion: Regarding the enemy's goals in a particular game, we expect him to behave rationally (that is, according to *our* logic): to be motivated in linear relation to the gains he expects from a win or draw; to head for a win only if justified by the position and/or strength of opponent; to behave in accordance with his objectives (fighting hard for a win; playing solidly and negotiating for peace when aiming for a draw).

By acting in a different manner, the enemy will try to *surprise* us.

Discussion

So far, we have treated 'intention' in its broader meaning, relating to our opponent's ambitions. Another way to view the phenomenon of 'intention', is in its short-term interpretation; that is, the intermediate goal of a series of moves.

Here we can meet the following types of surprise:

Routine moves, disguising non-routine intentions

See diagram 18.
12 h4

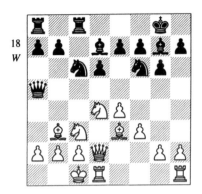

In this type of position, where kings find shelter on opposite wings, pawn-storms are the order of the day. In 99 out of 100 games, the intention of the text-move is to advance the outer pawn, to open the h-file for an attack by White's major pieces. However, there are other possible meanings for the pawn advance h2-h4!

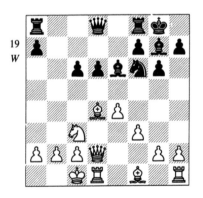

B. Lalić – Høi
Manila OL 1992

Black has sacrificed a pawn to open the b-file for his major pieces.

13 h4 ♕a5?

A standard reaction, but inappropriate here.

14 ♕g5! ♕d8

Regrettably, Black has to lose two tempi. 14...♕xg5+? 15 hxg5 would leave him with a weakness on h7 and no compensation for the sacrificed pawn. Note that White's 13 h4 was directed precisely against the queen sortie.

15 e5 ♘h5 16 exd6 ♗xd4 17 ♖xd4 ♕b6 18 ♕e5 ...with a considerable plus for White (1-0; 37).

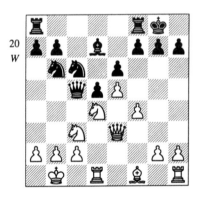

Larsen – Bareev
Hastings 1991

14 h4! ♖ac8 15 ♖h3 ♘a5 16 ♘b3!

Here the apparently aggressive 14 h4 was, in fact, a prelude to entering an advantageous endgame!

16...♕xe3 17 ♖xe3 ♘ac4 18 ♖f3 f6 19 exf6 ♖xf6

Or 19...gxf6 20 f5!.
20 ♘d4 ♖cf8 21 ♗xc4 ♘xc4 22 b3 ...with an edge (1-0; 40).

Another example of a natural move that conceals a surprising intention is the following:

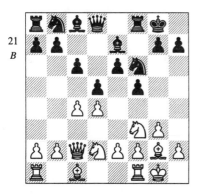

Black plays **8...♕e8**.
A standard move in the Dutch, aiming to transfer the queen to h5.

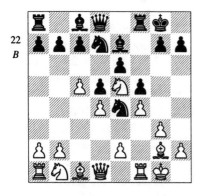

Chapman – Halliwell
England 1953

1...♕e8
The same move, but here Black has a vicious idea in mind...
2 ♘d2? ♘dxc5! 3 dxc5 ♗xc5+ 4 ♔h1 ♘xg3+ 0-1

Routine moves that conceal the existence of a far-reaching plan

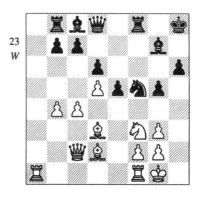

Hertneck – J. Polgar
Munich 1991

22 g4 ♘e7
After 22...♘h4? 23 ♘h2! Black's knight is doomed.
23 ♘h2 b5 24 ♗e4 ♗b7 25 ♖a3!
Hertneck's instructive comment: "Note that with his last moves, [White] has *silently and secretly* emptied the third rank for the rook... Black must always be on the watch for ♖h3 or even ♗xg5 with ♖h3".

The importance of camouflage is demonstrated here beautifully, each move being logical in itself: 22 g4 scared away the well-posted black knight; 23 ♘h2 provided a defence to the pawn on g4, and was apparently the start of a journey towards g3, eyeing the squares f5 and h5; 24 ♗e4 guarded d5 against future attacks. The enemy was given no clues as to the 'grand plan'.

25...♖f6? 26 ♖h3 ♔g8 27 cxb5!

...with a significant plus for White: d5 is taboo, in view of the pin along the a2-g8 diagonal (1-0; 39).

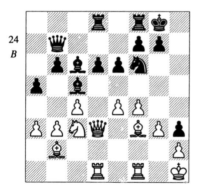

Grooten – Miles
Biel 1985

20...♖fe8!

"You would not think so" – grins the loser – "but the point of this move is ...♖e1#!".

21 g4? d5! 22 cxd5 exd5 23 exd5 ♘xd5! 24 ♘xd5 ♖xd5!

Now 25 ♗xd5 ♖d8 leaves White helpless. 25 ♕c3 is no help: 25...♖d4! 26 ♖xd4 ♗xf3+ 27 ♔g1 (27 ♖xf3 ♕xf3+ clarifies the preceding note) 27...♖e2! 28 ♖xf3 ♖xb2! winning.

25 ♕xd5 ♗xd5 26 ♖xd5 ♕a6 27 ♖fd1 ♖e3 28 ♖g5 ♕d3!

Avoiding the suicidal 28...♖xf3?? 29 ♖d8+ ♗f8 30 ♖xg7+.

29 ♖xg7+ ♔f8 0-1

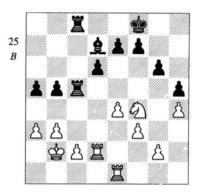

Anand – Kasparov
New York World Ch match (11) 1995

26...♔g7

This seemingly routine move, abandoning the defence of e7, masks a deep trap.

27 ♘d5 ♗e6!? 28 b4?

As subsequent analysis has shown, 28 ♘xe7 ♖e8 29 ♘d5 ♗xd5 30 b4! grants White a small advantage.

28...axb4 29 axb4 ♖c4 30 ♘b6? ♖xb4+ 31 ♔a3 ♖xc2!! 0-1

32 ♔xb4 ♖xd2 or 32 ♖xc2 ♖b3+ 33 ♔a2 ♖e3+ is hopeless.

B. Surprise in location

As mentioned before, spotting the enemy's intentions does not exclude surprise. One of the most common forms surprise can take, concerns the *place* where it is initiated. Here, too, we have to unearth our ulterior assumptions, in order to figure out what makes us disposed to surprise.

B1) Expected behaviour: **Movement of pieces will be directed (1) forward and (2) towards the centre.**

Recently I devised a simple experiment: I asked a subject situated in a square room to stand at point A (see illustration 1). His goal, he was told, was to reach two balls at the other side of the room. In the limited number of groups I tested, all subjects chose to move forward, towards the centre (see illustration 2). This is the most direct way, and the shortest. But it is certainly not the *only* way! Illustration 3 shows that there are other possible means of reaching the target. You will recognize these patterns when playing over the next set of chess examples.

Possible surprises

B1.1) Moving backwards

Dzindzichashvili – Sakharov
USSR junior Ch 1957
c3 Sicilian

1 e4 c5 2 c3 ♘f6 3 e5 ♘d5 4 d4 cxd4 5 cxd4 d6 6 ♘f3 ♘c6 7 ♗e2 ♗f5 8 0-0 e6 9 ♗d2 dxe5 10 dxe5 ♘db4 11 ♘c3 ♘d3 12 ♗g5 ♘xb2 13 ♕xd8+ ♘xd8 14 ♗b5+ ♘c6 15 ♘d4 ♗d3 *(26)*

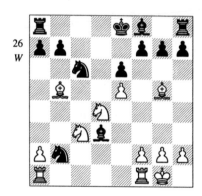

26
W

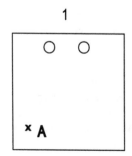
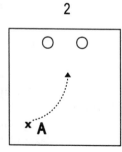
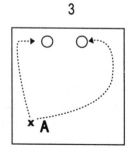

1 2 3

16 ♘xc6 ♗xf1 17 ♗xf1! bxc6 18 ♗c1 ♗a3 19 ♘b1! *(27)*

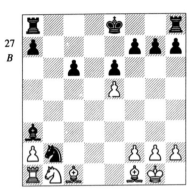

An artistic finale: White forced victory by retreating his entire army to base.

B1.2) Moving sideways

Pritchett – Ristoja
Groningen European
Junior Ch 1969/70
Modern Defence

1 e4 g6 2 d4 ♗g7 3 ♘c3 c6 4 ♗c4 d5 5 exd5 b5 6 ♗b3 b4 7 ♘ce2 cxd5 8 ♗d2! ♘a6 9 a3 bxa3 10 ♖xa3 ♘c7 11 ♕a1! a6 12 ♗a5! ♘f6 13 ♗a4+! *(28)*

A picturesque position. White enjoys a definite edge.

13...♗d7 14 ♖c3 ♖c8 15 ♘f3 0-0 16 ♗xd7 ♕xd7 17 ♘e5 ♕d8 18 ♘c6 ♕d7 19 ♘a7 ♘e4 20 ♘xc8 ♘xc3 21 ♘b6 and White wins material (1-0; 32).

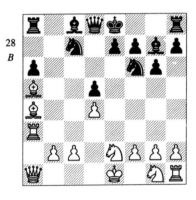

B1.3) Moving to and fro

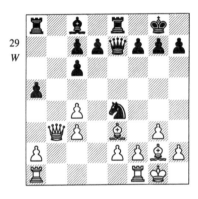

Ragozin – Lilienthal
USSR Ch (Tbilisi) 1937

13 ♖fd1 ♗a6 14 ♖d4! ♘c5

14...f5 is preferable. Now the rook will be useful along the *rank* as well as along the *file*.

15 ♕c2 ♘e6 16 ♖h4! *(30)*

16...♘f8 17 ♖d1 ♖ab8 18 c5

Black is left guessing as to precisely where White will deliver the death-blow.

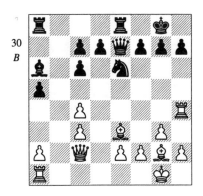

18...h6 19 ♖a4 *(31)*

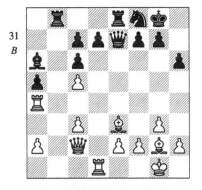

19...♗b5 20 ♖g4!

After 20 ♖xa5 ♖a8 Black obtains some counterchances. With the text, a divergence on the king's wing, White gains time to force matters in the centre or on the queenside.

20...♔h8

The most striking line is seen after 20...♘g6 21 c4 ♗a6 22 ♖e4 ♕d8 23 ♖ed4! *(32)* when the black centre collapses.

21 c4 ♗a6 22 ♕c3 1-0

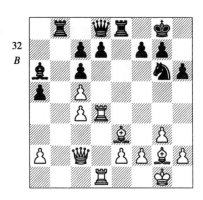

For a start, two black pawns disappear.

B2) Expected behaviour: **The main battle will take place where massive forces are concentrated.**

This could be rephrased as a reversal of cause and effect: the parties will mass their major forces where a collision is likely to occur.

Possible surprises

B2.1) Outflanking

See diagram 33 on the next page.
   43...♖b3

Black has a clear advantage, despite being a pawn down. With the following moves he increases his pressure.

   44 ♘c1 ♖b2+ 45 ♔g1 ♗e7 46 ♖b1 ♖xb1 47 ♘xb1 ♕b8 48 ♘c3 ♗c4 49 ♗f1 ♘xd4! 50 ♕xd4

   50 ♗xc4 ♗xc5.

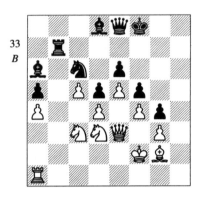

Soto Larrea – Ortega
Cuba 1953

50...♕a7! 51 ♘d3 ♗xd3 52 ♕xd3 ♗xc5+ *(34)* **0-1**

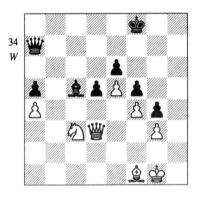

What has happened? It transpires that if 53 ♔g2 ♕h7!! then after all the wrestling on the queenside, the *coup-de-grâce* comes on the *king-side*! A spectacular finish.

In diagram 35 White enjoys a considerable space advantage and

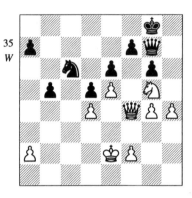

Matulović – Tsvetkov
Varna 1966

pressure on the weak point f7. However, the direct 32 h5 will not do, because of 32...gxh5 33 gxh5 ♘xd4+!.

Strangely, victory is gained on the opposite flank:

32 ♕c1! ♘xd4+

Otherwise the white queen settles on c7, molesting Black's queenside pawns.

33 ♔d3 ♕xe5 34 ♕c8+ ♔g7 35 ♕h8+! ♔xh8 36 ♘xf7+ ♔g7 37 ♘xe5

Yet another surprise, and the real point of White's combination: the black knight has no flight square.

37...♘f5 38 gxf5 gxf5 39 ♘c6 a6 40 ♔d4 ♔f6 41 f4 1-0

B2.2) Sneaking behind enemy lines

Wapner – Varga
Budapest 1994
Sicilian, Rossolimo

1 e4 c5 2 ♘f3 ♘c6 3 ♗b5 d6 4 0-0 a6 5 ♗xc6+ bxc6 6 h3 g6 7 ♖e1 e5 8 c3 ♗g7 9 d4 cxd4 10 cxd4 exd4 11 e5 dxe5 12 ♘xe5 ♗e6 13 ♘xc6

The beginning of an enterprising journey.

13...♕d6 14 ♕f3

Not 14 ♕a4? ♕d7!.

14...♖c8 15 ♘a7! (36)

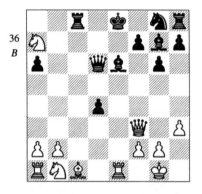

An heroic beast.

15...♖c5 16 ♗f4 ♕b6 17 ♕a8+ ♔d7 18 ♘c3!!

The justification of 15 ♘a7. Now on 18...dxc3, 19 ♖ad1+ is very powerful; and if 18...♘e7 then 19 ♘a4! is a killer.

18...♖xc3 19 bxc3 ♘f6 20 ♕f3 ♗d5 21 ♕d3 ♕xa7

The knight has loyally fulfilled its duty, but the time gained enables White's heavy artillery to join the battle.

22 ♗e5 ♘e8 23 ♕e2 ♗e6 24 ♖ad1 ♔e7 25 cxd4 ♔f8 26 d5 ♗f5 27 ♗b8!

White appears to be obsessed with this corner: 15 ♘a7, 17 ♕a8, and now this...

27...♕d7 28 ♕xe8+ ♕xe8 29 ♗d6+ ♕e7 30 ♗xe7+ ♔g8 31 d6 ♗d7 32 ♗h4 ♗f8 33 ♖e7! ♗xe7 34 dxe7 ♗e8 35 ♗f6 1-0

B3) Expected behaviour: **A player will try to gain an advantage in the area where he is stronger.**

In a lot of cases, the protagonists pursue independent strategies: White develops an initiative on the kingside, Black on the queenside (or vice versa); or one side gains control over certain squares, while the other gets a firm hold over an open file. It is as if both parties tacitly agree that neither will invade the other's territory and assets.

Possible surprises

B3.1) Invading the enemy's stronghold

See diagram 37.

Black's last move, 12...f7-f5, was designed to avert the break e3-e4 once and for all. Well...

13 ♖ae1! ♕b4 14 e4!!

This break, at an apparent fortified point, has reappeared in analogous positions in recent years. The black monarch stays in the centre, and White tears open his defences.

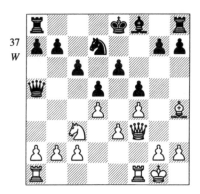

K. Richter – Baratz
Prague Olympiad 1931

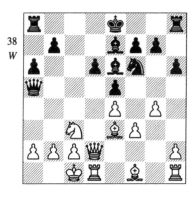

Shirov – Lutz
Munich 1993

14...dxe4 15 ♘xe4 fxe4

15...♕xd4+? 16 ♗f2 fxe4 17 ♕h5+ g6 18 ♗xd4 gxh5 19 ♗xh8 and White wins.

16 ♕xe4 ♕d6 17 ♕f5! ♕xd4+

17...e5 18 dxe5 ♕g6 19 ♕h3 is more stubborn, but White's attack prevails in any case.

18 ♔h1 ♗e7 19 ♕xe6 0-0-0 20 ♗xe7 ♖he8 21 ♕h3 ♕xb2 22 ♗xd8 1-0

See diagram 38.
14 a3

One is normally advised not to move the pawns around one's king, but here the move is connected with an interesting idea.

14...b5 15 h4 b4 16 ♘d5 ♗xd5 17 exd5 ♖b8 18 ♔b1 ♗d8?

Protects his queen and prepares 19...bxa3; nevertheless, a faulty move.

19 axb4 ♖xb4 20 ♕c3!

A star move, threatening 21 ♗d2 with a most annoying pin.

20...0-0

20...♖a4 21 ♕xa5 ♖xa5 22 ♗c4 is not much fun either.

21 ♗d2 ♖a4 22 b4! ♕c7

22...♕b6 23 ♕b3 traps the rook.

23 ♔b2!

The queenside, which just a few moves ago was the launching pad of Black's activities, has now been transformed into a death-bed for his troops. Black is helpless against ♔b3, capturing the rook.

23...♘xd5

Or 23...♕d7 24 ♕c6.

24 ♕xc7 ♗xc7 25 ♔b3 ♘b6 26 ♗e3 a5 27 c3 axb4 28 ♗xb6 1-0

C. Surprise timing

One of my childhood memories harks back to 1964, when the sports-world witnessed Sonny Liston, the ex-world heavy-weight boxing champion, losing his fight against Cassius Clay (later known as Muhammad Ali).

It was not the outcome that was shocking, but the course of battle. In heavy-weight professional boxing, antagonists generally compete for many rounds (up to fifteen), each round lasting three minutes. Now, in this particular fight, Clay did not beat around the bush: as soon as the gong was heard, he pounced on Liston and punched him with all his might. The battle was over in a knockout within two minutes; it was one of the shortest duels on record.

Pressing for victory, Clay was sure to attack his rival. But he was not expected to do it *so soon*!

In chess (and in other sports), the real fight does not normally commence at the very start. At the onset of the struggle the two parties gradually organize their armies, in preparation for the clash. Beginners who try for a Scholar's Mate are told that this is too direct a method, that an attack should be well-founded, and that the deployment of troops should precede attempts at annihilation.

Expected behaviour: **The commencement of chess combat is but an overture to forthcoming events. The real fight will flare up after a while, when development is complete and the respective forces have occupied suitable outposts.**

Graphically, this expectation is charted in illustration 4. A player is expected to take action when his forces are ready. *No sooner, no later.*

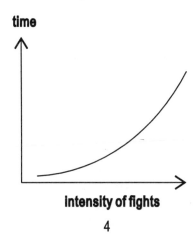

intensity of fights

4

Possible surprises

C1) Early assault: Heading for a smashing blow from the very first moves.

This type of surprise features in gambit play, or in a quick advance of the h-pawn, opening lines on the kingside. It can also be achieved by building an offensive structure, as in the following example.

Mukhin – Katalymov
Tashkent 1979
Spanish, Berlin

1 e4 e5 2 ♘f3 ♘c6 3 ♗b5 ♘f6 4 0-0 ♘xe4 5 ♖e1 ♘d6 6 ♘xe5 ♗e7 7 ♗d3 0-0 8 f4!? ♘e8 9 ♘c3 ♘xe5 10 fxe5 d6 11 ♘d5 dxe5 12 ♕h5

There is no sophistication in the way White deploys his army; he is quite blunt about his aims.

12...f5

If 12...g6 13 ♕xe5 ♗d6/f6?, then 14 ♕xe8!.

13 ♖xe5 ♗f6

13...♗d6 14 ♗c4!.

14 ♘xf6+ ♘xf6 15 ♕h4 c6

15...♖e8 seems better.

16 b3

Continuing the same naïve and direct approach: all White's forces are targeted at the black king.

16...♕b6+ 17 ♔h1 ♘e4?

Losing by force.

18 ♗c4+ ♔h8 19 ♗b2! ♘f2+ *(39)*

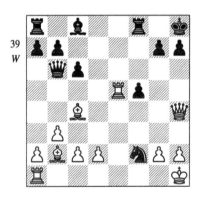

39
W

20 ♕xf2! ♕xf2 21 ♖e7 h5

Or 21...♖g8 22 ♗xg7+ mates.

22 ♗xg7+ ♔h7 23 ♗d4+ 1-0

C2) Abrupt change of modes: Occasionally, the character of a position is transformed: a positional battle becomes tactical; a middlegame turns into an endgame, etc. The accelerated pace of such a transformation is in itself capable of generating surprise.

Yandarbiev – Zagalov
1985
Caro-Kann, Classical

1 e4 c6 2 d4 d5 3 ♘d2 dxe4 4 ♘xe4 ♗f5 5 ♘g3 ♗g6 6 h4 h6 7 ♘f3 ♘d7 8 h5 ♗h7 9 ♗d3 ♗xd3 10 ♕xd3 ♕c7 11 ♗d2 ♘gf6 12 0-0-0 e6 13 ♘e4 0-0-0 14 g3 ♘xe4 15 ♕xe4 ♘f6 16 ♕e2 *(40)*

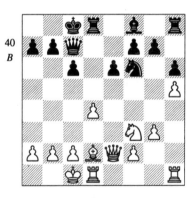

40
B

So far, ordinary play; nothing to write home about.

16...c5?! 17 ♖h4! cxd4 18 ♖xd4 ♖xd4 19 ♘xd4 a6?

White has gained some initiative, but after this mistake (19...♘d5 was correct) he develops a crushing assault.

20 ♗f4! ♛b6

20...♛c5 21 ♘xe6!.

21 ♛c4+ ♛c5 22 ♘xe6! *(41)*

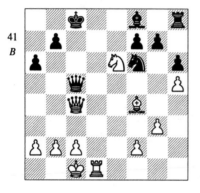

1-0

C3) Delayed action: Deferring the offensive, although the required resources for an immediate operation are available.

Research indicates that hesitancy by the aggressor, whether premeditated or not, tends to deceive the defender, thus facilitating surprise.

See diagram 42 opposite.

White's two bishops give him a minute advantage. If he wants to make something out of them, he must try to open up some files. The obvious plan in such positions is the minority attack: the advance b4, a4, b5. However, Flohr is not in a hurry.

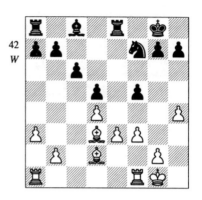

Flohr – Grob
Zurich 1934

21 ♖fe1 ♗d7 22 ♖e2 g6 23 ♗e1 ♚g7 24 ♗g3 ♖e7 25 ♖c1 ♖ae8 26 ♚f2 *(43)*

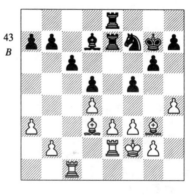

White has transferred his bishop to the important diagonal h2-b8, while his king and rook provide the necessary defence for his e-pawn.

26...h6 27 b4 a6 28 a4 ♚f6 29 ♖c3 ♖e6 30 ♗c2 ♖6e7 31 ♗d1 ♖e6 32 ♖b2 g5 33 ♗e2 ♚g6 34 ♗f1 *(44)*

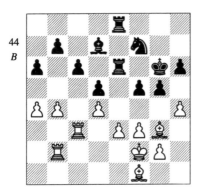

We shall pause to reflect upon White's play. Since the previous diagram, he has freed his kingside rook from its defensive duties; this now is the role of the queenside rook. The light-squared bishop has returned to its original post, not interrupting the co-operation between the other pieces. The advance b4-b5 is held in abeyance.

34...♖f6 35 hxg5 hxg5 36 ♗c7 ♘d6 37 ♗d3!?

Enabling his rival to simplify matters, but still keeping an edge.

37...♘e4+ 38 ♗xe4 fxe4 39 f4 g4 40 ♖c5 ♖f7 41 ♗e5 ♔f5 42 ♔g3 ♖h7 43 ♖b1 ♖g8 44 b5 axb5 45 axb5 ♖a8 46 bxc6 ♗xc6 (45)

47 ♖cc1!

It is time to regroup again, in this slow-motion picture. White now gains control over the more important open file.

47...♖a3 48 ♖e1 ♖f7 49 ♖a1 ♖xa1 50 ♖xa1 ♖f8 51 ♖h1 ♗d7 52 ♖h5+ ♔g6 53 ♖g5+ ♔f7 54 f5

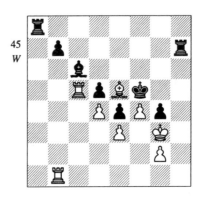

The end is approaching. Predictably, White bides his time.

54...♔e7 55 ♔f4! b5 56 ♖g7+ ♔d8 57 f6 b4

White has only one worry left: the enemy's passed pawn.

58 ♖h7 b3 59 ♖h1 ♗b5 (46)

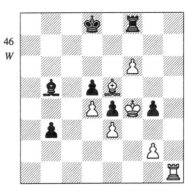

60 ♖b1! ♗c4 61 ♖a1! ♔d7 62 ♖a4

The final regrouping. The rook will stop the passed pawn from behind.

62...♔e6 63 ♖b4 ♖a8 64 ♖b7 ♖e8 65 ♔xg4 ♗e2+ 66 ♔f4 b2 67

🖺xb2 ♗h5 68 🖺b7 ♗d1 69 g4 ♗e2
70 🖺h7 ♗d1 71 g5 ♗e2 72 g6 ♗b5
73 f7 🖺f8 74 ♗g7 1-0

White never really attacked his
adversary! Looking back, it is difficult to pinpoint a critical moment
where Black erred.

D. A Doctrinal Surprise

Chess being a thoroughly investi-
gated and researched subject, a surprise in doctrine is most difficult to
achieve. It is exceptionally hard to
contrive completely new schemes of
development, let alone new tactics,
in our ancient game.

Admittedly, some changes have
occurred in basic chess theory: a
bishop is nowadays preferred to a
knight (not long ago, they were considered equals); the advantage of the
first move is recognized and backed
statistically; certain computer-dis-
covered positions require adaptation
of the 50-move rule...

Nevertheless, a revolution on the
scale of Steinitz's principles, or the
hypermodern school (Breyer and
Réti), is not likely to recur. Modern
concepts tend to take a more diffi-
dent form, of a local nature: a new
twist in a fashionable variation of a
familiar opening; a changed verdict
in a five- or six-piece ending...

Expected behaviour: **The enemy
will act according to: (1) the table**
**of pieces' relative value; 2) estab-
lished principles of development;
and (3) accepted positional principles.**

Possible surprises

*D1) Opting for disadvantageous
material imbalance*

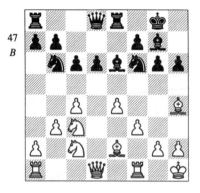

Khuzman – Yurtaev
Tashkent 1987

**14...♘xe4!?! 15 ♗xd8 ♘xc3 16
♕d2 🖺axd8**

Note that Black embarked on this
variation voluntarily: the queen sacrifice was not obligatory at all.

**17 🖺ae1 c5 18 ♘e3 d5 19 cxd5
♘bxd5 20 ♘xd5 🖺xd5 21 ♕c1 b5**
with ample compensation (½-½, 25).

As Burgess (1995) notes, the same
Yurtaev repeated a similar sequence
in a later game. Presently, others followed suit, trading a queen for two
minor pieces and just one pawn.

Naturally, after a while, such sacrifices cease to surprise. But on their first appearance, their effect is often thunderous.

D2) Devising a new interpretation to well-known schemes

Korchnoi – Khuzman
Beersheba 1993
Exchange Grünfeld

1 d4 ♘f6 2 c4 g6 3 ♘c3 d5 4 cxd5 ♘xd5 5 e4 ♘xc3 6 bxc3 ♗g7 7 ♗b5+ c6 8 ♗c4 b5 9 ♗b3 b4 10 ♗b2!? bxc3 11 ♗xc3 ♘d7 12 ♘f3 ♘c5 13 ♗c2 ♗a6

Preventing short castling, apparently casting doubt on White's preceding plan.

14 ♕d2 0-0 15 h4 h5 16 ♘g5 ♕d7 17 0-0-0! *(48)*

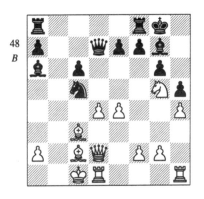

So, this was White's intention: castling long, accompanied by a pawn storm on the kingside, is rare in the Grünfeld Defence because of the danger presented by the g7-bishop.

17...♘e6 18 ♗b3 ♘xg5 19 hxg5 ♖ab8 20 ♖h3 ♕b7 21 ♕e3 ♕b5 22 f4 e6 23 ♕f2 ♖fe8?

Correct was 23...♕e2. Now the white attack gains strength.

24 ♖d2 ♗f8? 25 g4! hxg4 26 ♖h1 ♗g7 27 ♕h4 c5 28 f5 exf5 29 ♕h7+ ♔f8 30 ♕xg7+! 1-0

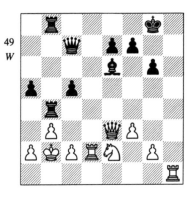

Sutovsky – Kudrin
Philadelphia 1993

White has a very promising position, but the direct 25 ♕h6? enables Black to defend with 25...♕e5+ 26 c3 ♖4b6, when the queen functions like a Dragon bishop.

25 c3! ♖4b6 26 ♘c1!

Protecting b3 and clearing the way for ♖d2, in order to join his colleague on the h-file.

26...a4 27 g4 axb3 28 a3!

A fantastic conception: the white king shelters behind a *black* pawn!

Now White is free to carry out his own attack.

28...♗c4 29 ♖dh2 e5 30 ♕g5 1-0

D3) Developing a playing-style that diverges from common methods and principles

This can be accomplished on a small scale, for example by assigning lesser, or greater importance to a certain principle.

"In [some] games, Short had deliberately mutilated his own pawn-structure ... In the seventeenth game he voluntarily saddled himself, right out of the opening, with a pawn structure so ugly that it reduced visiting grandmasters to shudders of disgust ... Short had been experimenting (in his preparations) with just such a provocation" (in Lawson, 1993, describing the match Kasparov-Short).

A doctrinal alteration can be confined to a certain game, or tournament. One explanation for Zsuzsa Polgar's overwhelming victory over Maia Chiburdanidze, in the ladies world championship Candidates' final 1995 (5½-1½) is the following:

"The key to victory lay in two surprises Polgar prepared for her opponent: playing, uncharacteristically for her, in an aggressive style; and choosing opening systems that she had almost never used." (Shutzman, 1995).

D4) Another kind of surprise takes place when encountering a player with a unique, peculiar style.

An example – the style of Ulf Andersson

In the old days, players concentrated on attack. Means of defence were not yet well-developed. Indeed, the whole concept of defending against the enemy's plots was regarded as dishonourable; gambits were – had to be – accepted, on principle; it was not a brave man's business to indulge in what was associated, in people's minds, with passivity and avoidance of positive action.

Naturally, the modern player's view is different. We all recognize the importance of good defensive skills. However, subconsciously, defence is still regarded as a **temporary** expedient (until the time comes to switch over to attack), a chore **imposed** upon us by the transient requirements of particular positions.

Only a handful of players choose **defence as a way of life**, aiming at defensive, restricted positions. The Swedish GM Ulf Andersson is a notable representative of this group.

See diagram 50 on the next page.

As Botterill confessed, at this juncture he felt very happy with his position. Black is faced with the advance 16 b5, and if 16...axb5 17

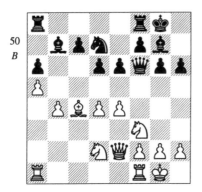

50
B

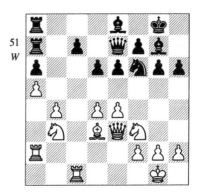

51
W

Botterill – Andersson
Hastings 1978/9

♗xb5, then he would be confronted with the positional threat 18 a6, driving the b7-bishop home.

15...♖a7!

Now 16 b5 fails, because after 16...♖fa8!! the a5-pawn will prove to be a weakness rather than a strength.

16 ♕e3 ♕e7 17 ♖a2!? ♖fa8

"It is quite extraordinary that Black can afford to pile up his rooks, apparently inactive, in one corner of the board like this" (Botterill, in Harding, 1982).

18 ♘b3 ♘f6 19 ♗d3 ♗c6 20 ♖c1 ♗e8 *(51)*

21 h3 ♖b7 22 ♕e1 ♕d8 23 ♘a1 ♗f8

Like no other player, Andersson uses his back ranks for waiting manoeuvres.

24 ♘c2 c5! 25 d5?

Failing to find a promising plan, as his idea of b4-b5 came to nought,

White sacrifices a pawn, but does not get sufficient compensation.

25...exd5 26 exd5 ♘xd5 27 bxc5 ♖e7 28 ♕d2 dxc5 29 ♗c4 ♘c7 30 ♕xd8 ♖xd8 31 ♘e3 ♔g7

...and Black won.

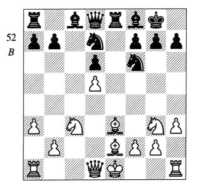

Kasparov – Andersson
Moscow 1981

13...♖xe3!? 14 fxe3 g6 15 0-0 ♕e7 16 ♕d4 ♗g7 17 ♕f4 ♘e8

In return for the exchange, Black is assured of good piece-play and a firm control of the key square e5. One presumes that he will try to attack the weak e3-pawn. However, as the game progresses, we witness Black apparently doing nothing active!

"Black's plan [is] not altogether usual: *voluntarily to spend the entire game defending*" (Polugaevsky and Damsky, 1988).

18 ℤac1 ♗e5 19 ♕f2 ♘df6 20 ♗d3 h5 21 ♘ge2 ♘h7 22 ♘f4 ♘f8 23 ♘b5 a6 24 ♘d4 ♗d7 25 ℤc2 ♗g7 26 ♕g3 ℤb8

Black's ongoing strategy is oriented towards parrying his enemy's potential threats. 20...h5 was a precaution against a possible g2-g4-g5 advance. Later, ...♘f6-h7-f8 was designed to guard g6. His last move supplied a defence to the b7-pawn. It can be quite depressing for a player to face an opponent who takes precautions even against his future, potential plans.

27 ℤe2 ♘f6 28 ♘f3 ♗e8 *(53)*

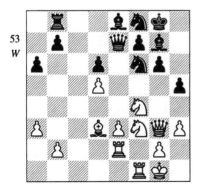

29 e4 ♘6d7 30 ℤc2 ♘e5 31 ♘xe5 ♗xe5 32 ♕f2 ♘d7 33 b4 ♕d8 34 ♗e2 ♗g7

...and the game ended in a draw on move 83.

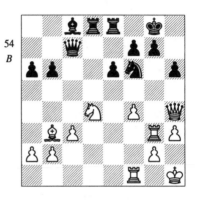

Adams – Andersson
Biel 1991

Here White has created some concrete threats, but Andersson stays calm and concentrates on mobilizing defensive recruits.

23...♔h8 24 ℤe1 ♗b7 25 ℤe5 ℤg8 26 ♔h2 ♕d6 27 ♗c2

Tries like 27 ℤeg5 or 27 ♗xe6!? were suggested after the game, but it appears that Black can hold his own in either case.

27...♕f8 *(55)*

In a position where one side is apparently so passive, it is rare that the other side can prepare his breakthrough in leisurely fashion, and yet be unable to find a convincing way through the defence.

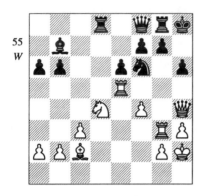

Annotating another Andersson game, GM Seirawan expressed his amazement: "Andersson seems to know exactly how far he can bend without breaking" (1990), realizing the bounds of the risks he can undertake.

28 ♖e2?

Adams recommends 28 ♖ge3 or 28 ♗b3.

28...♖d5 29 ♖g5 ♛b8 30 ♔g1 ♛d8 31 ♖xd5 ♛xd5 32 ♗b3 ♛d6 33 ♖d2 ♛c7 34 ♖d1 ♖d8 35 ♛f2 ♗d5 36 ♖e1 b5 37 ♗xd5 ♖xd5 38 ♛e3 ♔g8

The attack has evaporated. Black remains with a slight plus, due to his superior pawn structure. Play continued:

39 ♞f3 ♞d7 40 ♞e5? ♞xe5 41 fxe5 a5! 42 ♖e2 ♛c4 43 a3 ♖d3 44 ♛f2 ♖d1+ 45 ♖e1 ♖xe1+ 46 ♛xe1 ♛d3! 47 b3 ♛c2 48 b4 a4 49 ♛e3 ♛a2 50 ♛d3 ♛xa3

...and Black won on move 60.

E. Surprise in technology

The conduct of war is governed by tacit rules: there are things you can do, and there are things you cannot or, anyway, are not expected to do (like harming women and children). Even *total* war has its limitations: unconventional means are regarded as unacceptable, outside the realm of 'fair play'.

Expected Behaviour: **One's opponent's moves will be drawn from a reservoir of familiar theoretical ideas and combinational motifs.**

Possible Surprise: Usage of new, or rare weapons can generate surprise.

Four types of such weapons, in the context of a chess game, are illustrated below:

E1) Novelties in the opening

When commentators refer to surprise in chess, this is their most common example.

In the modern era, an opening novelty is frequently a one-time shot. After its first appearance, the innovation may get published and become common knowledge, hence losing its unexpected, unfamiliar features.

Since the topic is well covered in literature, we shall content ourselves with two examples and move on.

A. Feurstein – J.E. Bennet
USA corr. 1953
Fianchetto King's Indian/Grünfeld

1 d4 ♘f6 2 c4 g6 3 g3 c6 4 d5!? cxd5 5 cxd5 ♕a5+ 6 ♘c3 ♘e4 7 ♕d4 ♘xc3 *(56)*

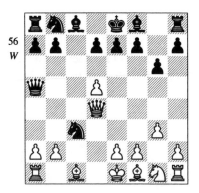

At the time this correspondence game took place, the variation was evaluated as advantageous for Black; Pachman gave 8 bxc3 ♖g8 with 9...♗g7 to follow.

8 ♗d2! ♕xd5 9 ♕xc3 ♘c6

White was threatening mate in one. If 9...f6 10 ♕xc8+ ♔f7 (with the double threat 11...♕xh1 and 11...♕xd2+!), then 11 ♘f3!, preventing both, wins.

10 ♕xh8 ♘d4

An attempt to fish in troubled waters. 10...♕xh1 fails to 11 ♗h6.

11 ♖c1 ♕xh1 12 ♕xd4 ♕xg1 13 ♕xa7! 1-0

M. Ashley – A. Shabalov
New York 1993
Exchange French

1 e4 e6 2 d4 d5 3 exd5 exd5 4 c4 ♘f6 5 ♘c3 ♗b4 6 ♗d3 c5 7 ♘e2 ♘c6 8 cxd5 ♘xd5 9 dxc5 ♗g4 10 0-0 ♗xc3 11 bxc3 ♘xc3 *(57)*

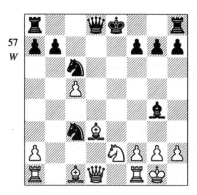

All this had happened in a game Waitzkin-Shabalov earlier that year. There White chose the continuation 12 ♕e1 ♕xd3 13 ♘xc3+ but after 13...♗e6 14 ♕e3 ♖d8 Black obtained a fine game (0-1, 27).

White's twelfth move appears to be compulsory, for example Black wins after either 12 ♕d2? ♗e2 13 ♗xe2 ♕xd2 or 12 ♕c2 ♗e2 13 ♗xe2 ♘d4.

12 ♕c2! ♗xe2 13 ♖e1! ♕d4

13...0-0? 14 ♗xh7+ ♔h8 15 ♕xc3 nets a pawn.

14 ♗b2 0-0-0 15 ♗f5+ ♔c7?! 16 ♗xc3 ♗d3 17 ♕c1 ♕c4 18 ♖e4! ♘d4

Or 18...♗xe4 19 ♕f4+.

19 ♕f4+ ♔c6 20 ♗xd4 ♖d5 21 ♗xg7 ♕xc5 22 ♖c1 1-0

Let there be no misunderstanding: the majority of opening novelties are not crushing in nature. Rather, their effect is enhanced (more precisely, *multiplied*) by the confusion they wreak in the enemy camp.

E2) Surprise tactics

Basic tactical themes are well-known and few in number: forks, pins, double attacks, square and line clearances, obstructions, deflections and some others. A tactical surprise occurs either by using really rare tactics, or by implementing an original version of a well-known motif. There follow some examples.

E2.1) Rare ideas

See diagram 58 opposite.

12 ♗h6?

An ordinary move that is countered energetically and decisively:

12...♘bc4! 13 ♕g5 e5! 14 ♘de2

Or 14 ♕xd8? ♗xh6+.

14...♗f6! 0-1

15 ♕g3 ♗h4 is amusing, but not for White.

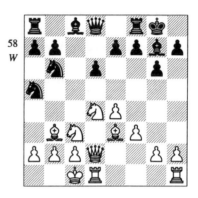

Fuchs – Honfi
corr. 1962

The length of a combination is not an essential element of surprise, as the following one-movers will testify:

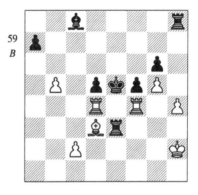

NN – Mannheimer
Frankfurt 1921

After **1...♖e4!** Black ends up a piece ahead.

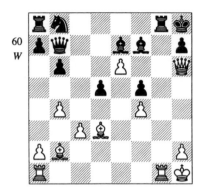

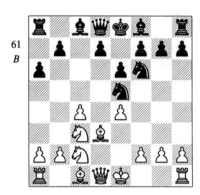

S. Hawes – S. Kerr
London Lloyds Bank 1979

Mabbs – Mohrlok
1959

26 ♗e4!!

This move wins. White avoids 26 c4+? d4+!, when it is Black who wins. After the text-move, 27 c4+ is not to be denied (26...♘c6 27 ♗xd5).

In order to create surprise, an idea doesn't have to be profound. Its scarcity value and efficacy are more important.

See diagram 61 opposite.
8...♕c7 9 ♕e2?

Disliking 9 b3 (9 ♘e3!) 9...b5!, he walks into a mine.
9...♕d6!

Most unusual, but totally crushing. As 10 ♔d2 ♘xc4+ 11 ♔e1 ♘e5 is unplayable, White tried 10 ♘d5 in despair (0-1, 16).

E2.2) Rare variations of familiar themes

Next we look at fresh variations of a worn-out concept: the *pin*. Although the basic idea is familiar to every novice, the combinations below have an original flavour, and their occurrence constitutes a surprise.

E2.2.1) Multiple pin

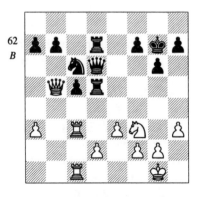

Y. Kagan – L. Shmuter
Israel 1995

26...♘d4!! 27 exd4 cxd4 28 ♖c5 ♖c7!!

Pinning on the file, as well as on the rank. White continued 29 ♖xc7 ♖xb5 and succumbed on move 45.

Returning to the position after Black's 26th, White can diverge with 27 ♘xd4 cxd4 28 ♖c5 but then 28...♖c7!! 29 exd4 b6 wins just the same: 30 ♕b2!? bxc5 31 dxc5+ ♕f6.

E2.2.2) Exchange of pins

Dembo – Ratner
Paris 1926
Alekhine Defence

1 e4 ♘f6 2 e5 ♘d5 3 ♘c3 e6 4 ♘f3 ♗e7 5 ♘xd5 exd5 6 d4 0-0 7 ♗d3 d6 8 0-0 ♗g4 9 h3 ♗h5 10 ♖e1 ♘c6 11 c3 ♖e8 12 ♗f4 dxe5 13 dxe5 ♗xf3 14 ♕xf3 ♗g5 15 ♖ad1 ♗xf4 16 ♕xf4 ♕e7 17 ♕g3!

The e5-pawn looks secure.

17...♘xe5

Fearing the advance of the white f-pawn, Black walks into a dangerous pin.

18 ♖e3! *(63)*

Not 18 f4? ♕c5+.

18...f6 19 f4 ♕c5! 20 fxe5 ♖xe5

Notwithstanding his material advantage, White is so tied up that he is hardly able to move.

21 ♖e1 ♖ae8 22 ♔f2 g5

Anticipating the freeing manoeuvre ♕g3-f4-d4.

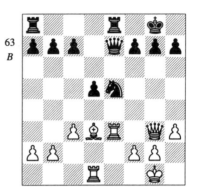

23 b4 ♕b6 24 ♕f3 ♔g7 25 g4 ♖8e7 26 a4 a6 27 ♖e2 *(64)* ½-½

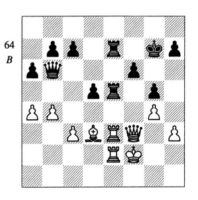

E2.2.3) Self-disruption of pin

See diagram 65 on the next page.
26...♖g6

"My opponent rose from his seat" – recalls Yosha – "under the impression that the game was over".

27 ♘f1!! ♗h3 28 ♘g3

Now if Black plays 28...♗xg2, the bishop blocks his rook, enabling 29 ♘xh5 (29...♗f3+ 30 ♘g3).

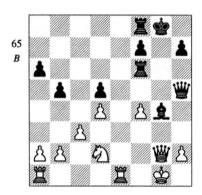

A. Yosha – T. Haines
Berlin 1983

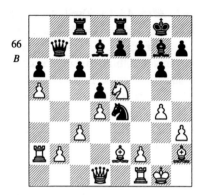

Polugaevsky – Gufeld
Moscow 1979

Objectively, Black still has a strong initiative. However, stunned by White's resource, he played badly and lost (1-0, 37).

E3) Choice of an off-beat weapon

Sometimes the enemy pursues ordinary schemes by employing rare (at least for him) weapons. A defensive player may play aggressively; a player with a tendency for combinations suddenly heads for a technical endgame; and so on.

See diagram 66 opposite.
19...♗xe5!
GM Eduard Gufeld is known for his predilection for King Indian formations, and, even more, for his devotion to the g7-bishop. Hence his decision to trade this piece for a knight is surprising.

"The psychological basis of Polugaevsky's plan was: surely Gufeld won't decide to give up his favourite bishop" (Gufeld, 1994).

It proved very effective.
20 ♗xe5 f6 21 ♗h2 c5! with Black having the more comfortable game (0-1, 46).

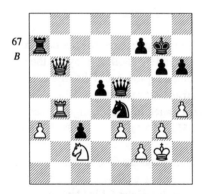

Winants – Kasparov
Brussels SWIFT 1987

42...♕f5 43 f3 ♘g5! 44 hxg5
♕xc2+ 45 ♔g1 ♕d1+ 46 ♔g2 ♕e2+
47 ♔h3 ♕xf3!!

One would think that in return for
his sacrificed rook, Black intends to
mate his rival's king...

48 ♕xa7 ♕h1+ 49 ♔g4 h5+ 50
♔f4 ♕f1+ 51 ♔e5 ♕f5+ 52 ♔d6
♕e6+ 53 ♔c7

Black wins after 53 ♔c5? ♕xe3+
54 ♖d4 c2.

53...♕e7+ 54 ♔b6 ♕xa7+! 55
♔xa7 (68)

68
B

It transpires that the decisive role
is played by another 'player': the advanced c-pawn; and that the combination commencing on Black's 47th
was aimed at ... exchanging queens!

55...c2 0-1

See diagram 69 opposite.
White is a pawn down, but Black
has not finished his development.
We expect White to commence an
attack.

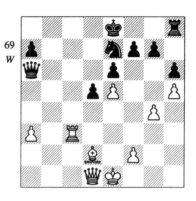

69
W

Makarychev – Naumkin
Moscow Ch 1983

28 ♖c7 ♕xa3

The threat was 29 ♗b4. Now 29
♕b1 0-0! 30 ♗b4 ♕f3! is unclear.

29 ♕c1!!

White opts for an *ending*, not a
mating attack!

29...♕xc1+ 30 ♗xc1 ♔d8 31
♖xa7 ♖e8 32 ♗a3 (70)

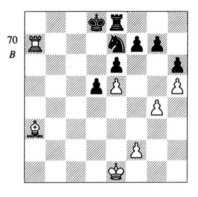

70
B

Zugzwang. Black is bound to lose
material when he runs out of moves.

32...f6 33 f4 fxe5 34 fxe5 ♘c6 35 ♖xg7 ♘xe5 36 ♗d6 ♘c6 37 g5 hxg5 38 h6 ♘d4 39 h7 ♘f5 40 ♗c7+ ♔c8 41 ♖g8 1-0

E4) Deploying non-chess weapons

As familiarity with *chess* weapons grows, the role of *psychological* coups increases. Psychological ploys often affect one's opponent's mood, his self-assurance, his equanimity, or his objective standpoint.

E4.1) Behaviour that shows contempt towards the enemy

E4.1.1) Being late for the start of the game

In the VSB tournament, Amsterdam 1996, the game Lautier – Kasparov began in a strange way: "Lautier turned up 5 minutes late for the game, and Kasparov 15 [minutes]. Evidently, this is a kind of ritual – who can arrive latest?" (Algra and Crowther, 1996)

E4.1.2) Making derogatory or lordly remarks about one's adversaries in public.

This can be done through a speech in a closing ceremony, in a journalistic interview, or simply by interspersing offending notes in annotations to a game.

"I always find it a pleasure to meet him in a tournament, since I had won my previous two encounters with him ... The move 1...c5 (in answer to 1 e4) showed me that Mr Adams was afraid of me and didn't know what to play ... In his first independent move in the game (13...b5) he commits a serious error ... [on move 37] Here he resigned, bringing my score against him to 3-0" (Tiviakov, commenting on his game against Adams, Groningen 1993).

Childish and inept as it may sound, such commentary may occasionally affect one's enemy in future battles; it is unexpected and confusing; one is not sure how to react to it.

E4.2) Behaviour directed to distract, annoy, or disinform the opponent

This weapon can manifest itself in a verbal or non-verbal interchange. It can take place before the match or during play.

Recently I learned that similar ammunition is used in tennis. "I'm really tired after last night, but I'll give it the old college try" is a characteristic warm-up ploy. Dressing extravagantly, or exuding confidence, are well-known in this sport (Weinberg, 1988), as they are in chess.

E4.3) Behaviour intended to inflict extra pressure on one's opponent

E4.3.1) Repeating the position

Nigel Short describes, through Dominic Lawson (1993), a common ploy of strong players: in a dominating position, they repeat the position twice, "partly to demonstrate that they were toying with their opponent and partly to tantalize him with the hope of a draw". He goes farther to dub this behaviour as a "sadistic trick".

E4.3.2) Lengthening the fight on purpose

This weapon is geared towards future fights with the same rival. In a game Ioseliani – Xie Jun from their women's world championship match in 1993, the Chinese player made the following comment:

"[in a won position] For psychological reasons I wanted the game to last as long as possible. I wanted to give her some hope, create the impression that there still were chances. Playing on in such a position in a match leaves a very bad memory".

These phenomena have become frequent in high-level chess. Some of these weapons border on the unethical, while other ploys are distinctly illegal. Unlike pure chessic weapons, they are rarely mentioned in instruction manuals, and thus may unnerve and surprise the unprepared.

Approaching the end of our survey, I feel that we have left aside a matter of great importance, namely:

Surprise in the Evaluation of Hostile Potential

Identifying the location of the clash between both armies, or the type of weapon in use, is secondary in significance to the following fundamental query:

Is our opponent capable of causing us serious damage?

Frankly, we have to admit that our answer to this query is occasionally negative. Either (A) our opponent is assessed as too weak to pose us problems; or (B) play results in a position that we consider solid enough to withstand an assault by (any) adversary.

It is my impression that quite a few chess surprises occur when a player simply *denies* the possibility of a negative result. Common expressions 'How could I lose to such a woodpusher?' or 'How could I have lost from such a position?' strongly support this view.

Underestimating the enemy's power: an upset by weak opposition

Every player is very familiar with this, having several painful experiences in his personal collection. Logically, we know that the stronger side does not always triumph; but psychologically, a 'rabbit' is often identified as someone incapable of inflicting pain.

Overlooking a position's hidden resources

A number of positions are deceptive in appearance. For example, we *feel* that there must be a win; we *believe* a winning path exists; we *know* that, for sure. But then a cold, objective analysis contradicts our instincts.

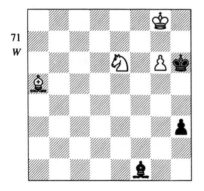

71
W

D. Gurgenidze, 2nd Prize,
Československý Šach 1973
White to play and win

1 ♔f7 h2 2 g7 h1♕ 3 g8♘+! *(72)*
Can this *win* for White?
3...♔h5
Alternatively 3...♔h7 4 ♘g5+ ♔h8 5 ♗c3#. With the text-move, the

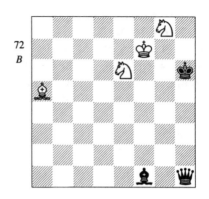

72
B

black king heads for the opposite corner...

4 ♘f6+ ♔h4 5 ♗e1+ ♔h3 6 ♘f4+ ♔h2 7 ♘g4+ ♔g1 8 ♗f2#

Yet his fate is the same. Black's queen and bishop self-block flight squares for their monarch.

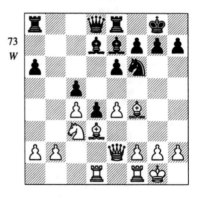

73
W

Murey – N. Grinberg
Ramat Gan 1980

The diagram was reached after the moves **1 e4 c5 2 ♘f3 ♘c6 3 d4 cxd4 4 ♘xd4 e6 5 ♘c3 a6 6 ♘xc6** bxc6 7 ♗d3 d5 8 0-0 ♘f6 9 ♗f4 ♗e7 10 ♕e2 0-0 11 ♖ad1 ♖e8 12 ♘a4 c5 13 c4 ♗d7 14 ♘c3 d4

White's position seems OK, but would you describe it as *winning*? Surprise lies here, as in the former example, in the *disparity* between the initial assessment and the ensuing play.

15 e5! dxc3 16 exf6 ♗xf6

16...gxf6 17 ♗xh7+ ♔xh7 18 ♕h5+ with 19 ♖d3 to follow is disastrous for Black.

17 ♗e4 ♖a7

17...♖c8 18 ♗b7 cxb2 19 ♗xc8 ♕xc8 20 ♗e5 is not easy for Black. Maybe 17...e5!? is somewhat better.

18 ♕h5! e5

Surprisingly, after 18...g6 19 ♕xc5 Black loses a whole rook.

19 ♕xh7+ ♔f8 20 ♗e3 ♕c8 21 b4! ♖c7 (74)

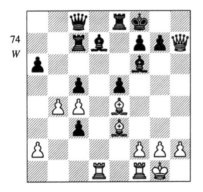

22 ♗b7!!

Charming. Now 22...♕xb7 23 ♖xd7 would be curtains.

22...♗f5 23 ♕h8+ ♔e7 24 ♗xc8 ♖xh8 25 ♗xf5 cxb4 26 c5 ♖b8 27 ♖d6 a5 28 ♖a6 ♖b5 29 ♖d1 g6 30 ♗c2 1-0

Bibliography

1. *Tigran Petrosian, His Life and Games* / V.C. Vasiliev / Batsford, London 1974

2. *Psychology in Chess* / N. Krogius / RHM Press, USA 1976

3. *The Psychology of the Draw Offer* / A. Fishbein / *Inside Chess* No. 5, 1993

4. *The Inner Game* / D. Lawson / Macmillan, London 1993

5. *Towards the Women's World Championship* / J. Shutzman / Schahmat No. 2, 1995 (in Hebrew)

6. *Why You Lose at Chess* / T. Harding / Batsford, London 1982

7. *The Art of Defence in Chess* / L. Polugaevsky and I. Damsky / Pergamon Press 1988

8. *The Mental Advantage* / R. S. Weinberg / Leisure Press / USA 1988

Quotations from Game Annotations

9. Kasparov – Anand / P. Wolff / *New in Chess* No. 7, 1995

10. Hertneck – J. Polgar / G. Hertneck / *New in Chess* No. 5, 1991

11. Grooten – Miles / H. Grooten / *New in Chess* No. 10, 1985

12. Sexy Chess Openings / G. Burgess / *Kingpin* No. 25, 1995

13. Tilburg 1990 / Y. Seirawan / *Inside Chess* No. 21, 1990

14. Yosha – Haines / A. Yosha / *Schahmat* No. 9, 1983 (Hebrew)

15. 10th VSB Tournament / J. Algra and N. Crowther / *Chess* No. 6, 1996

16. Tiviakov – Adams / S. Tiviakov / *New in Chess* No. 1, 1994

17. Ioseliani – Xie Jun / Xie Jun / *New in Chess* 1994

18. Polugaevsky – Gufeld / *My Life in Chess* / E. Gufeld / ICE, Seattle, USA 1994

4 Special Cases of Chess Surprise

Moving from the abstract to the concrete, is it possible to classify certain chess positions as 'prone to surprise'?

Well, yes and no. *It is* feasible to distinguish some chess phenomena that appear infrequently, have uncommon attributes and contain elements that contradict basic assumptions of chess players.

This, however, should be done with definite reservation: surprise possesses strong individualistic ingredients. What constitutes a shocking surprise for one, may be clear and obvious to another. Bearing this in mind, here are some positions that most of us would find surprising.

The target runs away

In diagram 75 Black has succeeded, by imaginative sacrificial play, to pose serious threats to the white monarch. By continuing 28...g4! he could cage in his king, when perpetual check would be inevitable. Instead, he tried for more with:

28...≡b8?

Intending 29...≡b2+ 30 ♔f3 ♕d1+ 31 ♔e4 f5+. However, the white king refuses to be a sitting duck and rushes forward:

29 ♔f3! ≡b2 30 ♔g4!

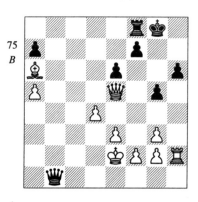

75
B

Plaskett – Hebden
England 1982

Now Black's attack is insufficient, e.g. 30...≡xf2 31 ≡xh6 ♕d1+ 32 ♗e2! ♕xe2+ 33 ♔h3 and White wins.

30...♕g6 31 ♗d3!

An echo of the previous note: the bishop commits suicide to deflect the black queen. Now 31...♕xd3 32 ≡xh6 and 31...f5+ 32 ♗xf5 both lose.

31...♕g7 32 ♕xg7+ ♔xg7 33 ♔f3 1-0

See diagram 76 on the following page.

Black devised a plan to put pressure on White's weak e-pawn:

24...≡e6 25 ♗f1 ≡fe8 26 ♗g2 ♘e7 27 f4 ♘f5!?

Carrying on with his plan, but...

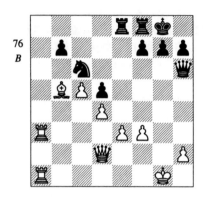

Hennigan – M. Gurevich
Philadelphia 1989

28 e4!! *(77)*

Black has laid siege to the backward pawn, but the dynamics of the position permit this very pawn to make a breakthrough!

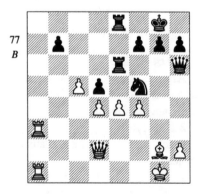

28...dxe4

Owing to the vulnerability of his back rank, Black cannot make an otherwise promising exchange sacrifice: 28...♖xe4 29 ♗xe4 dxe4 30

♖a8 ♕e6 31 d5 ♕d7 32 c6, etc.

29 d5 e3 30 ♕d3 ♖a6

After 30...♖g6 31 ♖a8 White's initiative clearly precedes Black's.

31 ♖xa6 bxa6 32 d6

32 ♕xf5 was a different path to victory.

32...e2 33 ♖e1 ♕xf4 34 d7 ♖d8 35 c6 ♘d4 36 ♕c3 ♘b5 37 ♖xe2! ♘c7 **38 ♕c5 ♖b8 39 ♖e1 g6 40 ♖f1 ♕h4 41 ♕e5 ♕d8 42 ♗d5 ♘xd5**

Now that the blockade is removed, Black collapses.

43 ♕xd5 ♕b6+ 44 ♔h1 ♖f8 45 ♖xf7 ♕b1+ 46 ♖f1+ 1-0

An immediate switch-back

Personal experience has taught me that a switch-back – returning a piece back to a square it had just vacated – is quite an unexpected scheme.

Bearing in mind the element of 'surprise in location', and our premise that direction of movement will be *forward*, an immediate switch-back appears paradoxical. I think you will agree that after White has just played, say, ♘h2-f1, the very last move his opponent expects is ♘f1-h2!

I've managed to execute this idea several times in my games. My opponents' reactions left no room for doubt: they were surprised!

In this complicated position (diagram 78), Black holds the advantage,

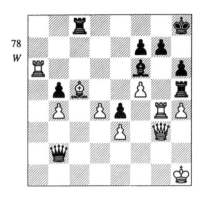

Avni – Porper
Israeli Ch 1992

due to the weakness of White's king-side pawns. 32 ♖f4? ♗g5! is bad.

32 ♖xf6!? ♖a8?

32...gxf6 is correct, when White has no time for 33 ♕d6? ♖xf5. Better is 33 ♕f4, though after 33...♕e2! 34 ♕xe4 (but not 34 ♗e7? ♖xh4+!) 34...♕f1+, with 35...♖xf5 to follow, Black has the upper hand.

With the text-move, Black hopes for 33 ♖xf7? ♖a1+ 34 ♕g1 ♖xg1+ 35 ♔xg1 ♕b1+ 36 ♔ any ♕a2+; 33 ♕g2 ♕a1+ 34 ♕g1 gxf6 35 ♖g8+? ♖xg8 36 ♕xa1 ♖xh4#; or 33 ♖xg7? ♖a1+ 34 ♕g1 ♖xh4#.

Oddly, it was precisely on Black's actual reply that I had counted, when playing 32 ♖xf6.

33 ♖a6!!

A common remark in game annotations is 'you should have seen his face when I played this move!'. Such was the case here.

33...♖xa6 34 ♕b8+ ♔h7 35 ♖xg7+ ♔xg7 36 ♕f8+ ♔f6 37 ♗e7+ ♔xf5 38 ♕xf7+ ♔g4 39 ♕f4+ ♔h3 40 ♕f1+ ♔g3 41 ♕f4+ ♔h3 ½-½

And here the same theme appears in a study:

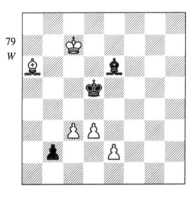

From a study by A. Avni,
Schakend Nederland 1978
White to play and draw

1 ♗c4+!! ♔c5

After 1...♔e5? 2 d4+ ♔f4 3 ♗d3 ♗f5 4 e3+ ♔g4 5 e4 it is Black who is in danger of losing.

2 ♗a6!! ♔d5

Black has two other plausible choices:

a) **2...b1♕** 3 d4+ ♔d5 4 ♗d3! with the double threat 5 e4# and 5 ♗xb1, and White manages to force a draw.

b) **2...♗f5** 3 e4! ♗xe4 4 d4+ ♔d5 5 ♗b7+ ♔c4 6 ♗xe4 ♔xc3 7 d5 ♔d4 draws.

3 ♗c4+!

Not falling for 3 d4?! ♗f5!, winning. The same trap existed, of course, on move one.

3...♔c5 4 ♗a6!

With a draw by repetition.

Recurrence of surprise

By definition, a certain surprise can take place only once: after that, it is surprising no more.

Sometimes, though, the same motif *does* recur in the same game ... if one's opponent operates under the impression that he can't be fooled twice ... then, paradoxically, he is bound to be surprised once again!

As a last resort, White starts a desperate attack:

21 ♖xg7+ ♔h8!

Both 21...♔xg7? 22 ♖g1+ and 21...♗xg7? 22 ♕xd8+ ♖xd8 23 ♖xd8+ ♗f8 24 ♗h6 lose.

22 ♖g8+ ♔xg8 23 ♖g1+ ♗g7 24 ♖xg7+

We have seen this before, haven't we?

24...♔h8!

Déjà vu. 24...♔xg7 25 ♕xe5+ ♔g8 26 ♕g3+ ♔f8 27 ♗h6+ ♔e7 28 ♕e5+ ♔d7 29 ♕d5+ draws by perpetual check.

25 ♖xh7+

Alas, 25 ♕f6 permits mate in one.

25...♔xh7 26 ♕h6+ ♔g8 27 ♕h5 ♕d1+ 28 ♕xd1 ♖xd1+ 29 ♔xd1 ♖c4 0-1

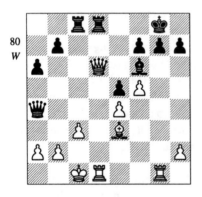

Tompa – Andruet
Bagneux 1982

A simple withdrawal of the white queen will lead to the fall of one of the unprotected pawns at e4 and a2. 21 ♕xf6? is foiled by 21...♖xd1+.

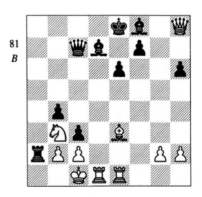

Bryson – Sher
Hastings 1996

21...♕a5!! 22 bxc3 bxc3 23 ♔b1 ♖b2+ 24 ♔c1 ♕a3 25 ♕xf8+ ♕xf8

**26 ♗c5 ♕g7 27 ♖d3 ♖a2 28 ♖ed1?
♕g5+ 29 ♗e3** (82)

29 ♔b1 ♖b2+ 30 ♔a1 ♖xb3 31 cxb3 ♕xc5 is winning for Black.

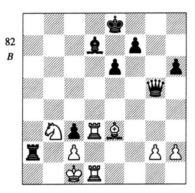

82
B

29...♕a5! 0-1

"Having overlooked Black's queen sacrifice the first time round, I managed to miss it again" commented the loser, ruefully.

Our final example of a repetitive surprise involves a suicidal piece.

See diagram 83.
1 ♖b5+! ♔c4

Forced, to avoid the loss of his queen.
2 ♖xb3! d3 3 ♖xd3!

The third successive offer of this rook. If it is left untouched this time, White will win prosaically.
3...♔xd3 4 ♘d4+ ♔xe3 5 ♗f5!

The stalemate defence is beautifully countered. The threat 6 ♘c2# decides the issue: White wins.

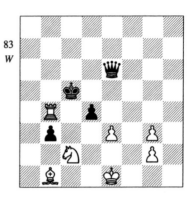

83
W

I. Shigapov, 2nd Honorable
Mention, *Rustavi* 1986
White to play and win

I have explained my reluctance to define and outline chess surprises in the first paragraph of this chapter. I am sure readers will enjoy – and be surprised by – *long moves* (diagram 84), *unforced king-moves in the opening* (diagrams 85 and 86) and the *helplessness of the queen* (diagram 87). Beyond that, I advise the reader to deduce from his own experience what kind of positions he finds surprising.

See diagram 84 on the next page.
Black has just sacrificed his queen. White's rejoinder casts doubt over this ploy.
28 ♕a1!!

A long move, with another long move in store.

28...♖hb8 29 ♔c1 ♖2b4 30 ♖c3! ♗b6 31 ♖b3! ♘xb3+ 32 axb3

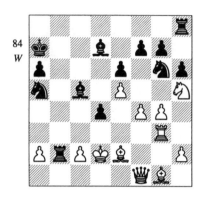

B. Perenyi – L. Portisch
Budapest 1988

Now the point of 28 ♕a1!! is revealed. With the aid of ♖g3-b3! (with a short break at c3), the frail black a-and d-pawns come under too much pressure.

32...a5 33 ♗c4 ♘e7 34 ♗xd4 ♘c6 35 ♗xb6+ ♖8xb6? 36 c3 ♖xb3 37 ♗xb3 ♖xb3 38 ♔c2 1-0

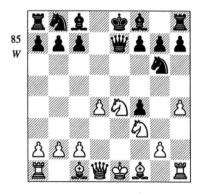

Spassky – Seirawan
Montpellier Candidates' 1985

With his last move, 7...♕d8-e7, Black assumes that the response 8 ♕e2 is obligatory.

8 ♔f2!

It transpires that 8...♕xe4 fails to 9 ♗b5+ ♔d8 10 ♖e1!. Once the capture is forbidden, the black set-up is inappropriate for future developments.

8...♗g4 9 h5 ♘h4 10 ♗xf4 ♘c6 11 ♗b5 0-0-0 12 ♗xc6 bxc6 13 ♕d3 ♘xf3 14 gxf3 ♗f5 15 ♕a6+ ♔b8 16 ♘c5 ♗c8 17 ♕xc6 ♖xd4 18 ♖ae1! ♖xf4 19 ♕b5+ ♔a8 20 ♕c6+ ♔b8 21 ♖xe7 ♗xe7 22 ♖d1 (1-0, 32).

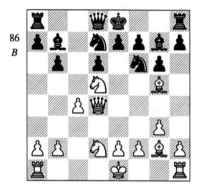

Reshevsky – Seirawan
Lugano 1987

The position arose after the moves **1 ♘f3 c5 2 c4 b6 3 g3 ♗b7 4 ♗g2 g6 5 d4 cxd4 6 ♕xd4 ♘f6 7 ♘c3 d6 8 ♘d5 ♗g7 9 ♗g5 ♘bd7 10 ♘d2.**

Black is under some pressure on the h1-a8 and a1-h8 diagonals.

10...0-0? loses to 11 ♘xe7(f6)+, while moves such as 10...♗xd5 and 10...e5 have obvious drawbacks.

10...♔f8!

An original and strong solution to the problems. Now Black threatens 11...♘xd5, since the g7-bishop is protected. Besides, 11 ♘xf6, being no longer *check*, allows 11...♗xg2.

11 ♘b3 ♘xd5 12 ♗h6 ♘7f6 13 ♗xg7+ ♔xg7 14 cxd5 e5! 15 ♕d3 ♕e8! 16 ♘d2 ♕a4 17 0-0 ♗a6 18 ♕e3 ♖ac8 and Black took over the initiative (0-1, 43).

See diagram 87.

1 h7 ♗xh7

1...♗e6 2 ♖e7! with the threat of 3 ♖e8+ draws, e.g. 2...♕xg6 3 ♖xe6 ♕g1 4 ♖f6+ ♔e7 5 ♖f7+.

2 ♖f7+! ♕xf7

Expecting 3 gxf7 g5, when Black wins.

3 gxh7!

Black's extra queen is useless and the draw is clear.

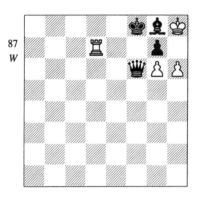

87
W

From a study by B. Gusev and An. Kuznetsov, special prize, *Tsereteli 150*, 1991
White to play and draw

Bibliography

Quotation from Game Annotation

1. Bryson – Sher / from *Chess* No. 4, 1996

5 More About Surprise in Chess

Effect of Surprise

Once a surprise has been unleashed, the play of the surprised party frequently suffers: an advantage gradually evaporates; an equal position becomes worse; mistakes abound.

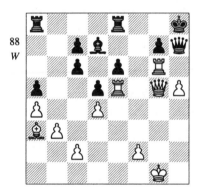

Ghizdavu – Timman
Jerusalem World Junior Ch 1967

If ever there was a completely winning position, it is the diagram position. White's pieces are ready for the final assault, while Black is powerless, with no counterplay.

33 h6

A safer winning method consists in trebling the heavy pieces on the g-file, and transferring the bishop to e5.

33...♖g8 34 ♗e7 ♕xh6!

A surprising move. Not that it saves Black: a miracle is required for that. Still, it is remarkable that Black can keep on resisting in a seemingly resignable situation.

35 ♕h5?

35 ♕g4! intending 36 ♖h5 clinches matters. 35 ♗f6 is less convincing due to 35...♔h7!. But what's wrong with the text-move?

35...♗e8!

The miracle has happened! Here White meditated for over half an hour, but found no way to repair the damage. A curious position.

36 ♕xh6+ gxh6 37 ♗f6+ ♔h7 38 ♖xg8 ♔xg8 39 ♖e3 ♗g6 (½-½, 63)

It is amazing what a single unforeseen move can do to one's confidence. The following examples, in which psychological blows affect pure chess reasoning, are typical.

See diagram 89 on the next page.

28...f5 29 ♕e2 ♖e7

Deflecting the queen, Black envisages a 'grand finale': 30 ♕xe7 ♘f2+ 31 ♔g1 ♘xh3++ 32 ♔h1 ♕g1+ 33 ♖xg1 ♘f2#.

Taken aback, White lost his fighting spirit and **resigned**. Instead, 30 ♖xh7+! forces perpetual check: 30...♖xh7 31 ♕e8+ ♔g7 32 ♕e7+

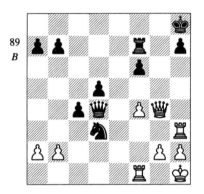

A. Carmel – Y. Grünfeld
Tel-Aviv 1989

♔g6 33 ♕g5+ ♔f7 34 ♕xf5+ ♔e8
35 ♕c8+ ♔e7 36 ♕c7+.

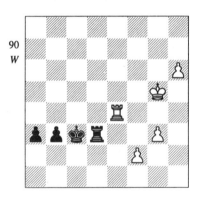

Sutovsky – Beim
Rishon le Zion 1994

Black has two advanced passed pawns; White has only one. The game is decided.

53 ♖e3 ♖xe3 54 fxe3 b2 55 h7 b1♕ 56 h8♕+ ♔d2

The situation has been transformed into a queen ending. The basic assessment remains the same though: White can throw in the towel with a clear conscience.

57 ♕d4+ ♔e2 58 ♕c4+ ♔f2 59 ♕f4+ ♔g2

Perhaps now is the time to call it a day?

60 e4! a2 61 ♕d2+ ♔h1 62 ♔g4

At this point Black must have been amazed: White keeps finding new counter-chances, even in this apparently barren position. This tends to have a negative influence on one's morale.

62...♕xe4+

62...a1♕ would subject the black monarch to a long series of checks. So, Black prefers a simpler path:

63 ♔h3 ♕f5+ 64 ♔h4 a1♕ 65 ♕e1+! *(91)*

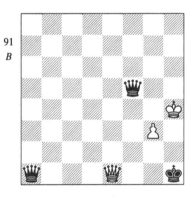

Oh dear! Where did this come from? Here Black, probably in a state of shock, agreed to a **draw**.

(65...♕xe1 is stalemate). In a calmer emotional state, he would doubtless have found 65...♕f1 (!!), winning easily.

Personality characteristics are closely related to the effect a surprising moment has on one's play. A player with a weak character may ruin an entire tournament following a shocking surprise. Tough, seasoned professionals do not allow themselves to fall apart, just for missing a single move.

An instructive case was described by ex-world champion, Mikhail Botvinnik. Playing against the rising star Bobby Fischer, he followed his prepared analysis, when a nasty accident occurred:

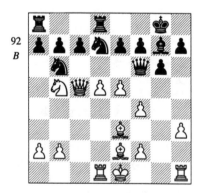

Botvinnik – Fischer
Varna Olympiad 1962

17...♕xf4!
Wins a pawn as 18 ♕xb6? loses to 18...♕e4 19 f3 ♕h4+ 20 ♗f2 ♕b4+.

"Suddenly it was obvious that in my analysis I had missed what Fischer had found with the greatest of ease at the board. The reader can guess that my equanimity was wrecked" (Botvinnik, in Fischer, 1972).

Yet the veteran fighter got over this major embarrassment and went on to put up tough resistance. He eventually drew the game!

Surprise and Risk

Chess is a game of continuous decision-making. Some of these decisions involve taking risks.

I believe that the concept of risk in chess is not fully understood. Authors have expressed strong opinions on the topic of sacrificial attack. But that is not synonymous with risk-taking.

Asked if he had certain rules as to when a player should sacrifice material in an attack, the late ex-world champion Mikhail Tal said:

"[In a discussion with GM Efim Geller] we generally agreed that in intuitive attacks there is a limit to the amount of material that can be sacrificed ... If for an attack on the king you have to give up a piece for one or two pawns, and there is the prospect ... of winning two pieces for a rook, then [you should go for it]. [However,] if you sacrifice a rook for a pawn, it would be good to be sure of at least perpetual check" (in Tal and Damsky, 1994).

Rudolf Spielmann, another brilliant attacker, stressed the relative value of pieces and the uselessness of prescriptions for successful sacrifices. Discussing the pros and cons of an exchange sacrifice over two full pages, he reached the not very helpful conclusion that practically, it all 'depends'. (Spielmann, 1935).

A major consideration when making a sacrifice is the *extent of risk involved*. Assessing it is frequently neglected in chess literature. Take, for instance, the next two episodes:

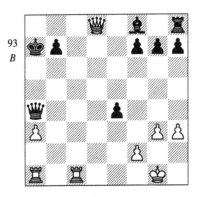

Leonhardt – Mieses
London match 1905

1...♗c5 2 ♕xh8 ♗xf2+ 3 ♔xf2?

3 ♔g2! ♕b3 4 ♕xg7 wins for White.

3...♕b3! 4 ♕d8 ♕f3+ 5 ♔e1 ♕e3+ 6 ♔d1 ♕g1+ 7 ♔d2 ♕f2+ 8 ♔c3 ♕c5+ ½-½

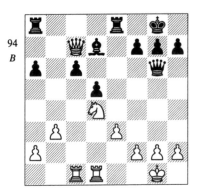

Zhukhovitsky – Petkevich
USSR 1968

1...♖a7 2 ♕xa7 ♗h3 3 ♔f1!

Not 3 g3? ♕e4 4 f3 ♕xe3+ 5 ♔h1 ♕f2 6 ♖g1 h5!, intending 7...♖e2!, when Black develops a powerful attack. After 7 ♕xa6 (7 ♖c2? ♗g2+!) 7...♕xd4 White is in difficulties, despite his material advantage.

3...♕xg2+ 4 ♔e1 ♕f1+ 5 ♔d2 ♕xf2+ 6 ♔c3 c5

Or 6...♖xe3+ 7 ♔b4.

7 ♕xc5 ♖c8 8 ♘c6

...and Black resigned shortly.

In both cases, Black sacrificed a great quantity of material. Both tries were objectively incorrect. The fact that in the first example Black gained success, is beside the point. Nevertheless, both sacrificial attempts were *totally justified*.

The reason for this seemingly contradictory assertion lies in the initial state of affairs: in both diagrams

Black is clearly in a hopeless situation and has *nothing to lose*. Remember what we have learned from military and international relations: the decision whether to take a risk should be evaluated with regard, *inter alia*, to the cost of taking no risk at all.

Pursuing this line of thought, the players with White in the two examples above should not have been surprised when their opponents initiated a desperate onslaught. Actually, this reaction should have been anticipated.

Be it in a clearly winning position, be it in a clearly losing position, the risk-dimension resolution is simple: take no risk when victory is in sight; opt for a high-risk strategy when an ordinary approach will not do.

Things are more complicated in double-edged positions, when the game's outcome is unclear. In such circumstances, when considering a precarious operation, a player should weigh relevant variables, such as alternative options, the desired outcome, both players' playing styles, the enemy's strength, and more.

In the following two cases, players took substantial risks in a dominating position. Such decisions are controversial. On the one hand, one is afraid to let an advantage slip by not being firm enough in keeping up the pressure. On the other hand,

risky actions may jeopardize victory: the gamble may lead to disaster.

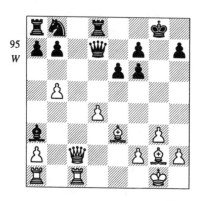

Boersma – Douven
Dutch Ch (Hilversum) 1985

20 ♕e4!

The simple 20 ♖d1 keeps a big plus: Black's queenside is weak and undeveloped; his kingside pawn formation is shattered; moreover, White holds the two bishops. Indeed, it should be possible to achieve victory by commonplace means.

High self-confidence and a tendency towards the romantic style in chess may have induced White to take this spectacular plunge.

20...♗xc1 21 ♖xc1 ♕xb5

From now on, it is all tactics: 21...a6 22 ♗h6 ♔h8 23 ♕f4 ♕e7 24 ♕g4 with mate to follow.

22 ♕g4+ ♔f8

Or 22...♔h8 23 ♗h6 ♖g8 24 ♗g7+, mating.

23 d5! ⟳d7

Guarding against 24 ♗c5+ ♔e8 25 ♕g8+.

24 d6! ⟳e5 25 ♗h6+ ♔e8 26 ♖c7 ♕b1+

26...⟳g6 27 ♕xg6 hxg6 28 ♖e7# is one way to go out with a bang. A similar variation occurs in the game.

27 ♗f1 ⟳f3+ 28 ♔g2 ♕xf1+ 29 ♔xf1 ⟳xh2+ 30 ♔g2 ⟳xg4 31 ♖e7#

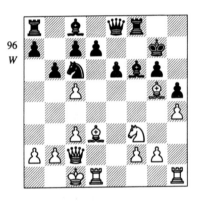

96
W

Stoltz – Colle
Bled 1931

In this opposite-wing castling position, things are not as clear-cut as in the preceding position. White is definitely on top: 17 ♕d2, a suggestion of Tartakower's, would have kept the edge, if not augmented it. Apparently, Stoltz wanted to finish off the game quickly:

17 g4?! hxg4 18 ♖dg1 ♗xg5+

Not co-operating with 18...gxf3? 19 ♗xg6! ♕xg6? 20 ♗h6+!.

19 ⟳xg5 ⟳e5 20 ♗e4

Asked to pick a colour, I believe the reader would still prefer White.

20...♗a6! 21 ♗xa8?! ⟳d3+ 22 ♔b1 ♕xa8

Jumping the fence with 22...♖xf2? backfires after 23 ♕a4!.

23 c4 ⟳e5 24 ♕c3 ♖f5 25 f4?!

Burning his bridges. If his assault fails, there will be no returning. Correct is 25 b3, with advantage.

25...gxf3 e.p. 26 ♖e1

The end?

26...f2! 27 ♖xe5 ♔g8!!

Not quite! Evidently, White reckoned only with 27...f1♕+? 28 ♖e1+!.

28 ♖f1?

28 ♖ee1 is the lesser evil.

28...♕g2 29 ♕d3 ♗xc4! 30 ♕xc4 ♖xe5 31 ♕d3 ♕xf1+ 0-1

In conclusion: We entertain certain beliefs about our rival's willingness to take risks. We do not expect him to go for bold sacrifices when it is possible for him to attain his goals by ordinary means. We predict that he will not play hazardously, if it is not his usual playing style. We believe that he will refrain from gambling, with its attendant uncertainty and excitement, if he is not highly confident in the outcome of his plan. We trust he will avoid dubious openings and dangerous experiments that have failed him in the past.

But if, contrary to our expectations, our opponent behaves differently, then surprise occurs.

Surprise, Deception and Warning Signals

In our survey of the theory of surprise, we saw that surprise is made possible through lack of early signs that signal to the enemy that something may be wrong.

A warning system may malfunction because a player is not as vigilant as he should be. He may also be lulled into a false sense of security by a cunning opponent who masks his intentions, or misleads him to adopt false premises.

Surprise, deception and (lack of) warning signals are closely related variables. I have treated the last two subjects in depth elsewhere[1]. Here we shall settle for a light illustration, for those readers who are unfamiliar with these themes.

See diagram 97.

26 ♗c3

The plan associated with this move, so it seems, is to dislodge the black queen from its post. 26...♗xc5? loses to 27 dxc5 ♕xc5 28 ♗b4.

26...♗c6? 27 ♗a5 ♕a7 28 ♕c1!!

Threatening not only 29 ♘xe6, gaining a pawn, but also the deadly 29 ♗d2!, capturing Black's knight in broad daylight. Watch how the innocent line-up ♕d2+♗c3 is transformed into the destructive ♕c1+♗d2.

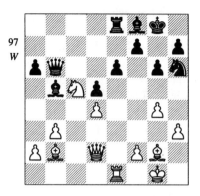

**97
W**

Timman – Khalifman
Amsterdam Donner Memorial 1995

28...e5 29 ♗d2 exd4 30 ♘d3 1-0

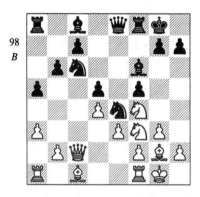

**98
B**

Bouwmeester – Pirc
1954

15...♘e7!

Shedding the c7-pawn to protect d5. Is this a desperate attempt to obtain some counter-chances, or a trap?

---

1   *Danger in Chess* / Amatzia Avni / Cadogan 1994

If it *is* a trap, what does Black get for this pawn?

16 ♕xc7? g5 17 ♘d3 ♗a6 18 ♘fe1

Trying to avoid the continuation 18 ♕c2 ♖c8 19 ♕d1(b1), in which Black develops some initiative, White plays into Black's hands.

18...♘c6!!

A skilful 'switchback' which entraps Her Majesty. One is reminded of certain animals that incite their victims to approach them, and then close their escape routes. The immediate threat is 19...♗d8, winning.

19 ♕xb6 ♗c4

This covers the flight-square b3, and threatens to win by 20...♖a6 21 ♕c7 ♖f7.

20 ♘c5 ♖b8 21 ♕c7 ♘xc5

Even stronger than 21...♖f7 22 ♘xe4.

22 dxc5 ♗e5 0-1

Evidently, *multi-purpose moves* (like Timman's 26 ♗c3 and Pirc's 15...♘e7) are ideal deceivers: the enemy is manipulated to assume that a move has been played with a definite goal, while in fact, its true object is completely different.

Graphically, this can be seen in the illustration below:

X, Y, Z and T are plausible ways to interpret the aims of move A. As the number of possible interpretations grows, the probability of our enemy picking a mistaken one increases (provided no clues are given).

Planning a surprise

Reading so far, it must have been clear that the author does not share the view that a surprise operation is something that just falls from a clear sky. On the contrary, it is (or should be) a planned action, carefully designed to disrupt the enemy's strategy, shaking his beliefs and expectations, thus undermining his self-confidence in the correctness of his assessments and in his overall abilities.

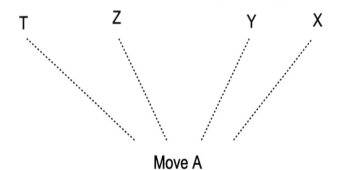

Move A

Strangely, annotators scarcely refer to the planning stage of surprise. The following description is, therefore, a piece of wisdom to treasure:

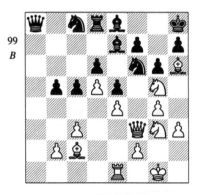

O. Bernstein – Dr Vidmar
St Petersburg 1909

"White's last move, 22 ♕d1-f3, revealed to me the opponent's intention to keep f7 under heavy pressure ... I knew that Bernstein was inclined to take any pawn not obviously poisoned; I also knew his predilection for 'elegant' sacrificial moves. My task was, therefore, to poison the f7-pawn in a manner not easily seen through, and at the same time encourage Bernstein to win it by means of a seemingly brilliant sacrifice" (Vidmar, quoted in Kirby, 1963).

Note the components of the plan: identifying the rival's intentions; taking the opponent's preferences and idiosyncrasies into account; luring him into action by presenting

him with an object; choosing a particular object that suits the enemy's playing style.

22...♘b6 23 ♔h2 ♖d7 24 ♖g1 ♘g8! 25 ♕xf7

This "brilliancy" was executed by Bernstein "without a moment's hesitation" (Vidmar). In fact, since the bishop at h6 cannot be protected, the move is forced.

25...♗f6!!

Suddenly the mating squares g7 and h7 are guarded, and the white queen finds itself trapped; the idea underlying Black's 22nd and 23rd moves is now revealed.

26 ♕f8

Black wins after 26 ♕e6 ♕d8.

26...♖e7 *(100)*

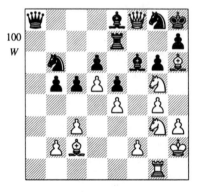

27 ♘e6 ♘d7 28 ♕xe7 ♘xe7 29 g5 ♘g8 30 ♘f5 gxf5 31 gxf6 ♘xh6 0-1

Later, Dr Emanuel Lasker pointed out that chess-wise, the result of Vidmar's 24...♘g8 was not overwhelming; from diagram 100, with 27 ♘h5!

♘d7 (27...gxh5?? 28 gxh5 ♘d7?? 29 ♘f7+! mates) 28 ♘xf6 ♘xf8 29 ♗xf8 ♕a7! 30 ♘xe8! ♖xe8 31 ♗xd6 White could have emerged from the chaotic intricacy with a position which was far from lost. But all this is irrelevant to our subject.

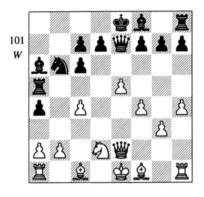

101
W

Shirov – Agdestein
Oslo 1992

13 ♖h2! f6?

As Black was soon to find out to his cost, the peculiar 13 ♖h2 was aimed against precisely this move.

14 exf6 gxf6 15 b4!! axb3 e.p.

What else? 15...♖h5? 16 g4 ♖h6 17 f5 is not appetising.

16 ♘xb3 ♖a4 17 ♘c5 ♕xe2+

Reluctantly, he settles for the loss of an exchange. 17...♖a5 18 ♘xa6 ♖xa6 19 c5 is worse (19...♘d5 is answered by 20 ♕xe7+ and then 21 ♗xa6).

18 ♖xe2+ ♔f7 19 ♘xa4 ♘xa4 20 ♖c2

...and White cashed in his material advantage (1-0, 38).

Readers may raise an objection: is the concept of surprise essential when expounding this episode? Isn't the old, familiar terminology sufficient here? Indeed, may it not be argued, simply, that White had set a *trap*, or conceived a pretty *combination*?

Well, I regard this standpoint as oversimplistic: the move 13 ♖h2 evolved from penetrating the adversary's mind, anticipating his intended 13...f6. After that, it was imperative to discover an unusual tactic that would rebut this idea. Thereafter, the link between a modest shift of a kingside rook and queenside expansion was hard to foresee. It certainly did not flow naturally from the characteristics of the position. Finally, the great speed in which developments unfolded after the surprising 15 b4!! afforded the black army no time to regroup. The fate of the battle was decided, literally, within a few moves.

The following endgame (diagram 103) has become a classic. In an analogous position, with colours reversed and with the omission of both h-pawns, Dr Emanuel Lasker won against Rubinstein, at St Petersburg 1914. A black win was expected here too, but during adjournment,

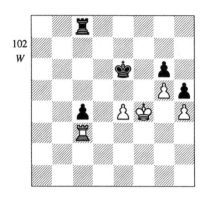

Botvinnik – Dr Euwe
Groningen 1946

Botvinnik discovered a marvellous saving idea:

41 ♔e3 ♔e5 42 ♖c2! c3 43 ♔d3

Now Euwe found out to his dismay that his intended 43...♖c7 would be met by 44 ♖xc3!! when the pawn ending after 44...♖xc3+ 45 ♔xc3 ♔xe4 46 ♔c4 ♔f4 47 ♔d4 ♔g4 48 ♔e5 ♔xh4 49 ♔f6 is only a draw.

In the game Black tried **43...♖d8+ 44 ♔e3 ♖d4 45 ♖xc3 ♖xe4+ 46 ♔f3 ♖xh4** but after **47 ♖c6!** was unable to win (½-½, 51).

Here we witness a case of pure chess means meeting ends; thus, no surprise weapons are required. Nevertheless, White deemed that an application of surprise could increase his chances of success:

"(Veresov and I) agreed that we would keep (our saving find) a secret – what if we were wrong? If the opponent got to know nothing of our analysis, then he would not be able to adjust to the new situation ... With downcast head I appeared in the hall ... (In answer to Euwe's greetings) I nod my grief ..." (Botvinnik, 1981)

In this episode we meet the *secrecy* component of surprise, and also a related factor: *deception*. Surprise was implemented as supportive tool, a *back-up* to a possible failure of chessic decisions.

Surprise in Defence

The notion of *surprise* is closely associated with the concept of *attack*. However, surprise can also be part of brilliant *defence*.

True, the range of possibilities is markedly confined in this instance: The defensive party must often respond to specific threats. All the same, brandishing implausible, unpredicted replies to the enemy's threats, is viable.

See diagram 103 on the next page.

The absence of dark-squared bishops tempts White to initiate an offensive against the black king.

16 ♘e4 ♕d8 17 ♕d2 ♔g7 18 ♖e3 ♘e7 19 ♖h3 ♘g8

White is allowed a free hand in developing his assault. Black's setup looks passive.

20 ♘g5 h6 21 ♗e4 ♖b8 22 ♕f4 ♗d7

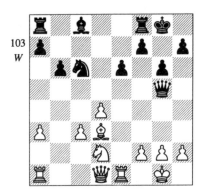

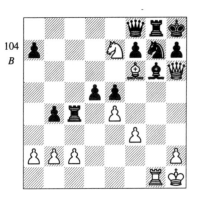

Krays – Kataev
Tel-Aviv Czerniak Memorial 1994

Calvo – Addison
Havana Olympiad 1966

Poor Black. No time to breathe, he is kept busy parrying White's threats. Right?

23 ♘f3 e5!!

A bombshell.

24 ♕xe5+ f6 25 ♕g3 g5

Naturally, 25...♗xh3?? permits mate in two. Now White is a pawn up, but his h3-rook makes a pitiful sight. Perhaps 26 ♖h5!?, with complications, was best here. Black can force a draw, if he likes (26...♗e8 27 ♖h3 ♗d7), or take some risks to win material (26...♕e8 27 ♘xg5!?).

26 ♗c2? ♖c8 27 ♘d2 ♗xh3 28 ♕xh3 ♖c7 29 ♕f5 ♔h8

...and Black realized his material advantage (0-1, 45). A strange affair: White made all the running – and then, suddenly, he was lost.

In diagram 104 White has sacrificed a rook to attain this promising position. His immediate threat is 29 ♖xg6! (29...fxg6? 30 ♘xg6#).

28...♖c6!!

An outstanding resource. If now 29 ♘xc6 (29 ♖xg6? ♖xf6! 30 ♖xf6 ♕xe7 is a win for Black), 29...♕d6! forces advantageous simplifications: 30 ♗xg7+ ♖xg7 31 exd5 ♕xd5, winning. In the game White chose another course:

29 ♘xd5 ♕c5 30 ♗xe5 ♕f2 31 ♕f4 ♖e8

And when Black disentangled himself eventually, his material superiority told (0-1, 46).

See diagram 105 on the next page.

With his last move, 17...♕e5-d5, Black has posed a serious problem for White. 18 ♖d1 ♗f5 19 e4 ♘xe4! 20 fxe4 ♗xe4 21 ♗g5 ♗xd3 22 ♗xd8 ♗xc2 23 ♖xd5 ♗xb1 is bad. An attempt to improve with 21 ♗xe4

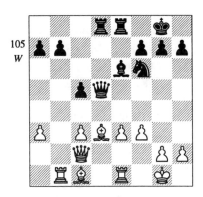

Najdorf – Unzicker
Santa Monica 1966

will not do because of 21...♕xd1+ 22 ♔f2 ♕g4! with a mighty attack.

18 ♗f1! ♗f5 19 e4 ♘xe4 20 ♕b3!

"A very surprising salvation. I count this among the most interesting moves I met with in my chess career" (Ivkov, 1968).

Indeed, the idea of refraining from recapturing a piece *that has captured material* is rare. From Najdorf's notes, one can surmise that he was as surprised as his opponent that his tactic worked! Play continued:

20...♘xc3

20...♕xb3 21 ♖xb3 ♘d6 22 ♖xe8+ ♖xe8 23 ♗f4! even favours White.

21 ♖xe8+ ♖xe8 22 ♕xd5 ♘xd5 23 ♖xb7 ♔f8 24 ♔f2

And White has full compensation for the pawn. The antagonists shortly agreed to a **draw**.

In our next example, surprise moves serve both in defence and in counterattack against the enemy king.

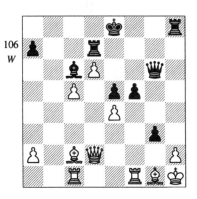

Matulović – Hurme
Helsinki 1981

Black threatens both 32...♖dh7, eyeing h2, and 32...♖g7, intending 33...g2+.

32 ♖b1! ♖g7 33 ♕g2 ♔d7

Defending against 34 ♖b8+, and threatening 34...gxh2 35 ♕xg6 (now not check!) 35...hxg1♕++ 36 ♔xg1 ♖xg6+.

34 ♗a4!!?

"[In acute time-trouble] played absolutely instantly" – marvels eyewitness GM John Nunn. 34 ♖xf5 ♕xf5 35 ♗a4 is a safe draw.

34...♖c8?

34...gxh2 35 ♗xc6+ (35 ♖b7+? ♔c8 36 ♖xg7 ♕xg7! wins for Black) 35...♔xc6 36 ♕xg6 hxg1♕++ 37 ♔xg1 ♖xg6+ 38 ♔f2 leads to an ending that White should hold.

35 ♗xc6+ ♖xc6 36 exf5 ♛h5 37 ♖b7+ (1-0, 42).

Surprise in the Endgame

I have not been able to detect many surprises in the final phase of the game. Upon reflection, this seems to be due to the fact that several assumptions, made during the opening and the middlegame, are not applicable to the endgame. Here, one generally does not expect a breakthrough, or a quick decision; it is also extremely difficult to conceive a new doctrine or unusual weapons, owing to the limited material.

As a rule, endings are conducted in positional, somewhat technical ways. One form of endgame-surprise is, then, use of tactical devices:

107
B

Ettlinger – Capablanca
New York 1907

1...♞c4!
A pawn sacrifice that paves the way to the king's invasion.

2 ♞xc4 dxc4 3 ♖xc4 ♚d5 4 ♖c8 ♚e4 5 ♖e8+ ♚d3 6 ♖xe2 fxe2+ 7 ♚e1

"At this point one would suppose that White could secure at least a draw. The actual termination is therefore a great surprise" (Dr Em. Lasker, in Brandreth and Hooper, 1975)

7...♗c7 8 ♗f4 ♗a5 9 ♗d2 *(108)*

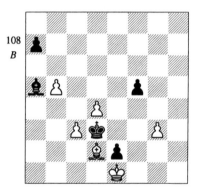

108
B

9...f4!!
This tactic had to be foreseen in advance.

10 gxf4 ♗d8 0-1

A mutual pawn race is a common occurrence in endings. The first side to promote almost always emerges victorious. Anomaly creates surprise.

In a bleak situation (see diagram 109), White makes a desperate bid to reverse the game's fortunes:

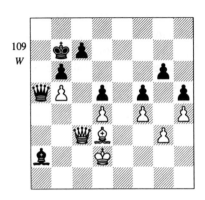

Davies – Khalifman
London 1991

45 ♕xa5 bxa5 46 g4!? hxg4 47 ♗xf5 gxf5 48 h5

Since Black's pieces are far away, this sprinter cannot be stopped. However...

48...g3 49 ♔e3 g2! 50 ♔f2 ♗c4 51 h6 a4 52 h7 a3 53 h8♕ a2 *(110)*

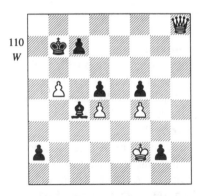

Despite trailing in the pawn race, Black has the last laugh: the squares a8 and h1 are guarded, while the promotion of his a-pawn cannot be averted.

0-1

A new theoretical finding in the endgame is rare. Chess computers have made some discoveries; they are interesting, but like the following position, have limited application to practical over-the-board chess.

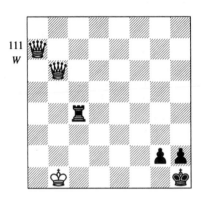

J. Pletanek and E. Vlasak,
5th Honorable Mention,
Bohemian RT 1983-4
White to play and win

White has two queens and Black has none, but curiously, it's not that simple. 1 ♕a8? ♖c1+! demonstrates the difficulty.

1 ♔b2!! g1♕ 2 ♕a8+ ♕g2+ 3 ♕f2!

Amusingly, the win is assured just when the balance of queens becomes equal.

3...♕xa8 4 ♕f1#

Generating Surprise by Habituation

Our opponent will be surprised when facing a move, or a plan, that seems impossible or unlikely to occur.

One way to reach such situations is to design a routine situation, where *repetitive* ordinary actions produce dynamics of *habit*. Our opponent will gradually become accustomed to constantly attending our threats in certain positions, and to recurring manoeuvres. Perceptibly, his alertness will wane. At exactly this point, our surprise has good chances to succeed.

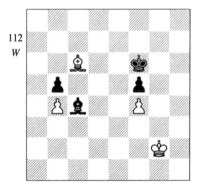

J. Pinter – B. Alterman
Beersheba 1991

The position is drawish; in fact, many a player would abandon a desire to win and split the point. Undeterred, White carried on:

99 ♗b7 ♗d3 100 ♔f2 ♔e7 101 ♗c8 ♔d6 102 ♔e3 ♗e4 103 ♔d4 ♔c7 104 ♗e6 ♔d6 105 ♗f7

White's only winning attempt consists of arriving at the following diagram position *(113)*, when it is Black's turn to move.

Reciprocal zugzwang

It is a zugzwang: a black bishop move loses a pawn, and a king move enables a decisive penetration by the white king. However, the position is *reciprocal zugzwang*: with White to play, it is a draw, since there is no way to keep the dominating position of the king and bishop and pass the move to Black.

So, Black must take care not to fall into this reciprocal zugzwang.

105...♗c6 106 ♗h5 ♗d5 107 ♗d1 ♗b7 108 ♗b3 ♗e4 109 ♗d1 ♗b7 110 ♗e2 ♗c6 111 ♗f1 ♗e8

Naturally not 111...♗d7?? 112 ♗d3! and White wins.

112 ♗g2 ♗f7 113 ♗f3 ♗e8 114 ♗d5 ♗d7 115 ♗g8 ♗c6 116 ♗h7 ♗d7 117 ♗g6 ♗e6 118 ♔d3

White has failed to make progress. With this strange move, he invites Black to fall into 118...♔d5?? 119 ♗e8!.

118...♗d7 119 ♗h5 ♗e6 120 ♔c3 ♔d5 121 ♗f3+ ♔d6 122 ♔d4 ♗f7 123 ♗g2 ♗e8 124 ♗b7

Haven't we been here before?

124...♗d7??

Finally Black tires of this apparently pointless messing around. Instead 124...♗f7 draws: 125 ♗c8 ♗g6 leads nowhere.

125 ♗d5!

Unexpectedly, a different reciprocal zugzwang! White forcefully brings about the winning scheme.

125...♗e8

Or 125...♗c8 126 ♗f3! ♗d7 127 ♗d1!, as in the game.

126 ♗b3! ♗d7 127 ♗d1! 1-0

127...♗e6 128 ♗e2 ♗d7 129 ♗d3 wins a pawn and the game.

Countering surprise

Surprisingly (*sic!*), first-hand evidence on the theme of countering a chess surprise is scant. Constructing hypothetical speculations, describing how player A avoided surprise in position x, is, I'm afraid, mere quackery. The best we can do, then, is to point out some theoretical, yet applicable, observations.

Before surprise is unleashed

It is worthwhile to sustain a frame of mind in which a surprise is likely to occur.

We should take into consideration that: 1) our opponent is constantly trying to outsmart us; 2) chess is extremely complicated, containing numerous options; 3) being human, there is a limit to what, and how far we can see ahead. It is only natural that ideas, plans and specific moves are overlooked, or incorrectly evaluated.

Once we come to terms with these facts of life, our future reaction to surprise will be less severe, confusion will not inflict a paralysis of mind.

Smelling an approaching surprise, a player may deviate from well-trodden paths.

Typical danger signals are: our opponent selects an unusual (for him) opening line; plays uncommonly quickly and confidently; or steers into a position evaluated by theory as inferior.

Obviously, if one has great confidence in oneself and is very familiar with the opening in question, one might not want to side-track.

In his pre-game preparations, a player may be wise to contemplate several scenarios.

By doing this, the likelihood of being surprised is, by definition, decreased.

Imagine one is playing a last-round game, with an opponent in a 'must-win' state. What will such an opponent's game-strategy be?

A useful list should probably include the following plausible alternatives:

- He will storm ahead from the very first moves.
- He will try to engage us in a long, manoeuvring battle, in an attempt to wear us down.
- He will concentrate his efforts on accumulating small advantages, hoping to overcome us in the endgame.
- He will be content with an equal position, assuming that a draw is undesirable for us as well as for him, provoking us to force matters.
- He will complicate, hoping that we err in the ensuing time-trouble.

Naturally, there are other scripts. One can't be sure which scenario will actually come true. But if one prepares for these five options, deciding *in advance* how to respond to each of them, one's chances of being caught off-guard are narrowed.

Specializing in certain areas in chess may deter our opponent from initiating a surprise in these areas.

If a player is reputed to be 'champion of the French Defence', or he is known for his illustrious tactical skills, then any future opponent will think twice before engaging him in these domains.

Admittedly, if one *does* concoct a surprise in one's opponent's pet line, or in a field that is supposed to be the enemy's expertise, it *is* going to be a real surprise (not that it is sure to guarantee success).

During occurrence of surprise

At the moment our opponent springs his (prepared) surprise, we are prone to a cognitive trap of *magnification* (Barns, 1989): a tendency to exaggerate one's problems and shortcomings, while underrating one's defensive resources.

Hence it is essential to remain cool-headed and keep calm. This opinion is held, *inter alia*, by GM Artur Yusupov. In a deep and interesting article, entitled 'Unexpected moves in the opening', he advises:

"A great deal depends on how quickly you recover and adjust your frame of mind to the full-blooded struggle. Mental disarray can lead to a quick collapse ... The main thing is not to lose your self-control ... not to lose your head, not to panic" (1994).

In the process of calming down, the technique of 'positive self-talk' is of great help. Listening to our inner voice, whether it transmits logical statements ('You haven't committed a single mistake, so your position is no worse'; 'He couldn't have thoroughly checked every variation'); or just supportive, encouraging fondlings of our ego ('You are a strong player, he will be sorry for playing this nonsense'; 'Hang on, everything will be fine') are typical confidence-builders.

After a surprise has been unleashed

The surprised party should give himself some time to recover from the initial shock.

Some players respond quickly to a surprising move, thus disguising their unpreparedness. More often, it is better to give oneself a pause for reflection, digesting the unexpected blow, evaluating its consequences.

Once a player recovers, he should proceed with his game as if everything were normal.

Some players carry on passively, trying to minimize the damage. Others resign themselves to an air of inevitable defeat. By doing this, they help the enemy. And then, there are others, who believe that just because they have failed to foresee the enemy's plan, there must be something

wrong with it. So, they set out to find a clear 'refutation' of his scheme.

Says GM P. Benko:

"When you find yourself on the receiving end of an opening surprise ... play sound developing moves! ... Searching for a sharp refutation over the board in an unfamiliar position would be asking for trouble ... [it] may not even exist. [You should] save time, and a lot of grief, by looking merely for healthy moves to keep the position in balance" (in Benko and Hochberg, 1991).

In conclusion of this section, let us present a rarity: a candid description of a player who found himself facing an unpleasant surprise.

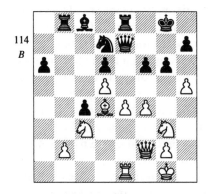

114
B

Pachman – Doda
Havana 1965

26...♖f8! 27 ♖e3?

White has fair compensation for his material deficit. However, his last move ignores a trap. Black grabs the opportunity:

27...♘e5!

"I was suddenly aware that my position was in ruins" – says Pachman. 28 fxe5 fxe5 29 ♕d2 exd4 30 ♕xd4 ♖xb2 loses. If the black knight remains untouched, it will land on d3 (assuming that the crude threat – 28...♘g4 – is prevented), eyeing b2 and f4 – a sad state of affairs.

"My first reaction was to consider immediate resignation ... but I then saw a glimmer of a chance: if ... ( ) ... then ... ( ). However, it seemed too slender a prospect that my opponent would readily fall in my plan ... Was there any way of 'bluffing' [him] into [my trap]? If I were in time-trouble, he might imagine that [my move] was a blunder ... In order to attempt this ploy ... I sat quietly at the board for a whole hour ... I allowed myself a mere three minutes for the remaining 13 moves ... Meanwhile, he was walking about on the stage, no doubt pleased with his position" (in Pachman, 1978).

28 ♕d2 ♘d3 29 ♘d1 ♘xf4? 30 ♘f5!

A happy ending. Black fell for this counter-surprise. Depressed, he committed more mistakes, and lost.

30...gxf5 31 ♖g3+ ♚h8 32 ♕xf4 ♖b3? 33 ♘c3 ♖xb2 34 exf5 a5 35 ♘e4 ♖e2 36 ♘xf6 ♖xf6? 37 ♕g5 ♖e1+ 38 ♚h2 1-0

Going back to the winner's commentary, we can clearly identify the phases he went through:

1) Shocked by surprise, his spirits fall.

2) Overcoming the bad feeling, he starts to examine the position, looking for counterchances.

3) Objectively assessing the situation, he devises a plan.

4) Regretfully, he concludes that his scheme does not stand much hope. To increase its chances, he searches around for another possible ingredient.

5) Subconsciously probing for tacit expectations, Pachman realizes that:

a) Black anticipates an easy victory;

b) A strange move by White will evoke suspicion, causing Black to probe into the position and most likely fathom his intentions;

c) A strange move by White, *while in time-trouble*, is likely to be considered a blunder.

6) Finally, White implements his plan very carefully, concealing any signs that may give his adversary reason to worry.

With all this, a significant co-operation from Black was required, in order to let White of the hook. Let us remind ourselves that the weapon of *surprise* can only *support* chess decisions, not replace them.

Bibliography

1. *Attack with Mikhail Tal* / M. Tal and I. Damsky / Cadogan, England 1994
2. *The Art of Sacrifice in Chess* / R. Spielmann / McKay, USA 1951
3. *Achieving the Aim* / M.M. Botvinnik / Pergamon Press, England 1981
4. Unexpected Moves in the Opening / A. Yusupov / in *Opening Preparation* / M. Dvoretsky and A. Yusupov / Batsford, London 1994
5. *Winning with Chess Psychology* / P. Benko and B. Hochberg / McKay, USA 1991
6. *The Good Feeling Handbook* / D.D. Burns / William Morrow, 1989

Quotations from Game Annotations

7. Bernstein – Vidmar / Kirby / *South African Chess Player* 1963
8. Najdorf – Ivkov / in *Second Piatigorsky Cup* / I. Kashdan (ed.) / Dover, USA 1968
9. Matulović – Hurme / J. Nunn / *British Chess Magazine* 1981
10. Ettlinger – Capablanca / in *The Unknown Capablanca* / D. Hooper and D. Brandreth / Batsford, London 1975
11. Pachman – Doda / in *Complete Chess Strategy, Part 3* / L. Pachman / Batsford, London 1978
12. Botvinnik – Fischer / in *My 60 Memorable Games* / R. Fischer / Faber and Faber, London 1972

6 The Way Players Experience Surprise

Throughout the book, one hindrance pops up time and again: the shortage of *authentic* accounts on chess surprises by the parties involved.

In an attempt to overcome this handicap, I have asked several strong players to choose a memorable game (or an episode from it), that is preserved in their memory as a surprising experience.

The following esteemed contributors [at the time of writing (1997), they are all rated above 2500 Elo] generously agreed to share with us their thought-processes during surprising moments. Their varied experiences should serve to enhance our understanding of the phenomena of surprise.

Eran Liss – Bela Lengyel
Budapest FS 1992
Ruy Lopez
Notes: GM Eran Liss

1 e4 e5 2 ♘f3 ♘c6 3 ♗b5 a6 4 ♗a4 ♘f6 5 0-0 ♗e7 6 ♖e1 b5 7 ♗b3 d6 8 c3 0-0 9 h3 ♘a5 10 ♗c2 c5 11 d4 ♕c7 12 ♘bd2 ♘c6 13 d5 ♘a5 14 ♘f1 ♘c4 15 ♘g3 g6 16 a4 ♗d7 17 b3 ♘a5 18 axb5 axb5 19 ♗g5 ♘b7 20 ♕d2 ♖fc8 21 ♘h2 *(115)*

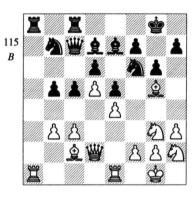

115
B

White has emerged from the opening with a marked advantage; he has a clear plan on the kingside (f4) while Black's play on the queenside is neutralized.

21	...	b4
22	c4	♖a3?!

Leading, eventually, to the loss of a pawn.

23	♖xa3	bxa3
24	♖a1	♖a8
25	♖a2	♕d8
26	♗e3	

Preferable is 26 ♘f3, reactivating the knight and saving a tempo compared to the game.

26	...	♖a6
27	♕c1	♕a8
28	♕a1	♘e8
29	♗c1	♘c7

30	♘f3	♗d8
31	♘e1	(116)

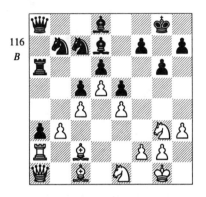

116
B

White drops his original kingside plan (21 ♘h2 intending f4), directing all resources at the queenside. Black, for his part, switches his efforts from the queenside to the other wing, seeking some play for the lost pawn.

31	...	♗h4
32	♖xa3	♗xg3
33	fxg3	f5
34	♖xa6	♕xa6
35	♕c3!?	

At this stage I thought that leaving the queens on board afforded better chances than entering an endgame.

35	...	fxe4
36	♗xe4	♘e8
37	♗h6?!	

Inaccurate. 37 ♗g5! was far better, completely paralysing Black.

37	...	♘d8
38	♘f3	

38 g4! is stronger.

38	...	♘f7
39	♗d2	♘f6
40	♗c2	♗f5
41	♗xf5	gxf5
42	♕a5!?	♕c8?!

Trading queens is the lesser evil.

43 ♘g5!

Suddenly the exposed black king is under powerful pressure. It is quite surprising that with scant material, White heads for an attack against the king. Interestingly, White changes direction once again: this time, from the queenside to the kingside.

43	...	♘xg5
44	♗xg5	♘e4
45	♗h6	♕d7

The threat was 46 ♕a7.

46	♕a8+	♔f7
47	♕f8+	♔g6
48	h4!	(117)

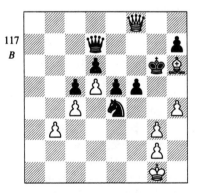

117
B

48	...	♘f6?!

Loses immediately, but the position cannot be held. A more stubborn defence against White's threat of 49 ♗e3, coupled with 50 ♕h6+, or 50 h5+ ♔xh5 51 ♕h6+ ♔g4 52 ♕h3#, was **48...♔h5** (not 48...♕f7?? 49 h5+ ♔f6 50 ♗g7+). Then 49 ♗g7!? ♔g6! 50 ♗h8!? h5! or 49 ♗e3 ♔g4 50 h5 ♔xg3 51 ♕g8+ (51 h6 f4 52 ♕g7+ ♕g4!) ♔h4 52 h6 f4 53 ♕g7 ♕g4! does not work. Correct is **49 ♔h2!**.

During the game I examined the continuation **49...♔g4** 50 ♕g8+ ♔h5 51 ♗e3 ♕e7 52 ♔h3 ♕d7 and failed to find a win. 53 ♗g1!? is very interesting: if 53...f4+ 54 g4+ ♔h6 55 g3!! Black is in zugzwang (55...♕e7 56 g5+ ♔h5 57 g4#). However, Black has an antidote: 53...h6! when the situation is unclear.

Further analysis shows that White can nonetheless win with **50 ♗g7!**; if 50...♘xg3 then 51 ♕g8 f4 52 ♕e6+ is decisive (52...♕xe6 53 dxe6 ♘f5 54 ♗f6).

By the way, diverging from this with 49...♘f2 will transpose into the game after 50 ♕g8!! ♘g4+ (not 50...♘e4? 51 ♗g7 and White wins) 51 ♔g1 ♕e7 52 ♗f8.

    49 ♗g5   ♘g4
    50 ♕g8+   ♔h5 *(118)*
    51 ♗h6!!

A key move in White's plan. The expression of surprise on my opponent's face was unmistakable.

    51 ...   ♕e7
    52 ♗f8   ♘h6
    53 ♗xe7   1-0

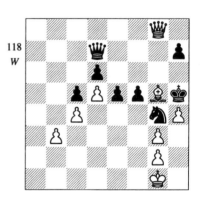

118
W

Discussion (by A.A.)

The game is rich in several manifestations of surprise.

A) *Surprise in intentions*

On move 35 White refrained from exchanging queens, despite holding a material advantage. Later (move 43), he turned his attention to the enemy's king, although at this stage the limited material did not favour such an operation.

B) *Surprise in direction*

White changed the direction of his forces' movement on several occasions, causing confusion in his adversary's camp.

C) *Switch-back moves*

The manoeuvre ♗g5-h6 was repeated time and again. All in all, the dark-squared bishop visited both squares three times.

D) *The target runs away*

This rare theme appears in variations that were left behind the scenes in this example (e.g. Black's possible defence with 48...♔h5 and 49...♔g4).

Guy Heller – Gad Rechlis
Beersheba Ch 1981
English Opening
Notes: GM Gad Rechlis

1	d4	♘f6
2	c4	c5
3	♘f3	cxd4
4	♘xd4	e6
5	♘c3	♗b4
6	♘b5	d5
7	♕a4	♘c6
8	♗g5	0-0
9	0-0-0	*(119)*

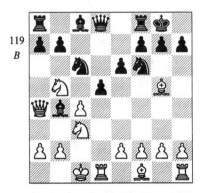

Now 9...h6 is a good move, but after five minutes' thought, I discovered the following devilish trap:

9	...	a6!
10	cxd5	exd5
11	♘xd5	axb5!
12	♕xa8	*(120)*

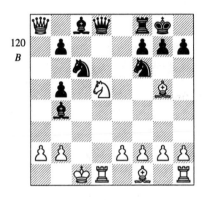

12	...	♕xd5!!

The last two moves came as complete shock to my opponent. I was only fourteen years old when the game was played; I still look at it with affection.

13	♖xd5	

Or 13 ♗xf6 ♕c5+ and wins.

13	...	♘xd5
14	a3	♗d6
	0-1	

Discussion (by A.A.)

After White's eleventh move, Black is a pawn down, and apparently suffers from two pins: on the h4-d8 diagonal, and along the a-file. Then, with two successive sacrifices, Black blasts his enemy. The *target* of his sharp combination is not the relatively exposed white king, but his queen! An ingenious tactical trick; in the final position White is defenceless against ...♘c7 or ...♘b6.

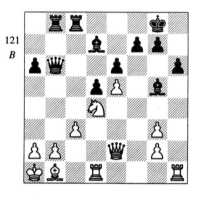

Yona Kosashvili – Gad Rechlis
Israeli Ch 1986
Notes: GM Gad Rechlis

In this position, which arose from an Open Sicilian, Black holds some advantage, but White's position appears solid.

```
23  ...      ♗a4
24  ♖df1     ♗e3!
```

The start of a series of startling moves. White should have prevented this bishop incursion by 24 ♖d3.

```
25  ♖h4      ♖c4
26  ♗d3      ♖xd4
27  cxd4     ♗xd4
28  ♖b1      ♗d1!! (122)
29  ♕d2
```

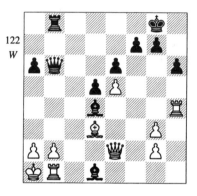

29 ♖xd1? ♗xb2+ 30 ♔b1 ♗a3+ wins for Black after either 31 ♔a1 ♕c7! or 31 ♗b5 ♕c5.

```
29  ...      ♗xe5!
30  g4       ♗b3!!
31  ♖h5      f5
32  ♖e1 (123)
```

32 gxf5 ♗xa2 33 fxe6 ♗xb1 34 ♖xe5 ♗xd3 wins for Black.

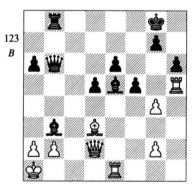

```
32  ...      ♗c2!!
```

A calm position (the one before Black's 23rd move), has given rise to a fierce sacrificial onslaught. I must

admit at being amazed at how everything went smoothly, 'like clock-
work'.

	33	♛xc2	♝xb2+
	34	♔b1	♛d4!
	35	a4	♝a3+
	36	♝b5	axb5
	37	♛b3	♝b4
	38	♖d1	♛xg4
	39	♖h3	bxa4

0-1

Following this game, Kosashvili
abandoned the Open Sicilian for a
while.

Discussion (by A.A.)

A bright game, which won the tournament's beauty prize. Each move in
itself is not exceptional: the theme of
deflection is a well-known tactical
device. However, some factors lend
this aesthetically pleasing attack a
surprising nature: the sudden change
in the position's character; the fact
that (almost) every tactic worked in
Black's favour (a surprise for both
sides!); the never-ending blows that
the black bishops inflicted upon
White.

Perhaps the disparity between
positional evaluation ('White is
slightly worse') and tactical calculations ('White loses by force') also
generates a sense of surprise.

The notes of the following game
are by GM Ronen Har-Zvi.

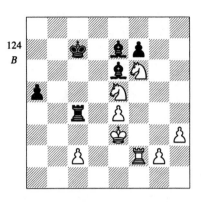

124
B

Yochanan Afek – Ronen Har-Zvi
Tel-Aviv 1996

Earlier in this game, my adversary had missed a chance to close
the queenside, thus assuring himself
a significant advantage. At the cost
of two pawns, Black opened up the
position. In the diagram, Black's
chances lie in the passed a-pawn,
aided by two raking bishops.

Now White had five minutes to
reach the time-control; and Black
only two or three.

	33	...	♝c5+
	34	♔d3	♖d4+
	35	♔e2	

Not 35 ♔c3? ♖d1! when White
must shed material to avert 36...♝d4#.

| | 35 | ... | ♖c4 |

Assuring the draw: what a relief,
having regard to past events. Weaker
is 35...a4 36 ♖f1 (36 ♘d5+? ♔d6!).

| | 36 | ♔d3 | |

36 ♘xc4? loses to 36...♝xc4+ 37
♔e1 ♝xf2+ 38 ♔xf2 a4.

36 ...   **♖d4+**
37 ♔e2 *(125)*

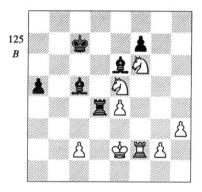

125
B

White accompanied this move with an offer of a draw, expecting 37...♖c4 38 ♔d3 with repetition. But after I had made my 35th move, I had found an interesting possibility:

37 ...   **♔d6!!**

One exclamation mark is for the move's *strength*; the other is for its excellent *timing*: just when White has reconciled himself to the idea that the game was heading for a draw.

38 ♘eg4

The only move. Both 38 ♘d3? ♖xd3! and 38 ♘f3? ♗c4+ 39 ♔e1 ♗b4+ lose outright.

38 ...   **a4**
39 e5+

39 c3!?.

39 ...   **♔c6**
40 ♘e3   **a3**
41 ♖f1   **♖b4**

41...a2 42 ♖a1 ♖b4 43 ♘ed5 complicates Black's technical job.

42 ♖a1

42 c3 ♖b2+ 43 ♔d3 ♗xe3 44 ♔xe3 a2 comes to the same thing.

42 ...   **♗xe3!**
43 ♖xa3

Or 43 ♔xe3 a2 followed by 44...♖b1, winning.

43 ...   **♗d4**

The e5-pawn falls; White's position is hopeless.

44 ♖a6+   **♔b5**
45 ♖a8   **♗xe5**
46 ♘h7?   **♖b2!**
47 ♔d1   **♗f5**
48 ♖e8   **♗f4**
49 ♘f6   **♗xc2+**
50 ♔e1   **♗d3**
51 ♘d5?

51 g4 was compulsory, though insufficient. Now White is mated.

51 ...   **♖b1+**

0-1

Discussion (by A.A.)

Black's 37th move combines surprise in *intention* (going for the full point, while two pawns down) with surprising *timing* (in mutual time-trouble, immediately after his opponent's offer of a draw). Maximum *effect* is ensured through a *misleading* operation (displaying an apparent willingness to aim for a three-fold repetition).

Earlier developments are pertinent: having missed chances to gain an edge (see Ronen Har-Zvi's initial comment) White regards a draw as an unsatisfactory result. Reluctantly, he comes to terms with it, only to realize that Black is intent on winning: a crushing blow.

Rafael Vaganian – Artur Kogan
Antwerp 1996
English Opening
Notes: IM Artur Kogan

1	♘f3	c5
2	c4	b6
3	g3	♗b7
4	♗g2	g6
5	d4	cxd4
6	♕xd4	♘f6
7	0-0	♗g7
8	♘c3	♘c6

I selected a line I had never played before: an unusual move-order leading to a known theoretical position, in which it is customary to proceed with 8...d6 followed by 9...♘bd7. Black's main problem in this line is that after he castles, White plays ♕h4, ♗h6, with an initiative on the kingside and in the centre.

The move I chose forces White to determine his queen's location: 9 ♕h4 is strongly met by 9...h6!, and 9 ♕f4 ♕b8! enables Black to solve most of his problems.

9	♕e3	0-0
10	♖d1	♕c8!
11	♗d2	♘g4
12	♕f4	f5! *(126)*

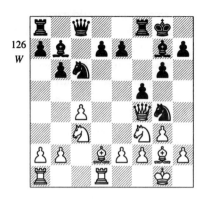

126
W

Following a surprising sequence of moves, White finds himself in a somewhat tricky situation. In order to defend against 13...♗h6, he reluctantly exchanges an important central pawn.

13	c5	bxc5
14	♕c4+	♔h8
15	♕xc5	d6
16	♕c4	♘a5!

Although Vaganian is reputed to be one of the best endgame players in the world, I believed that the ensuing queenless position offered me good chances.

17	♕xc8	♖fxc8
18	h3	♘f6
19	♘d4	♗xg2
20	♔xg2	♘c4
21	♗c1	♖ab8

A critical juncture. After my last move, I assessed the position as good for me, because of the harmonic and active co-operation of my pieces. Nevertheless, because of the weaknesses in Black's pawn structure (e7, a7), the e6-square could easily provide a splendid post for the white d4-knight. Another consideration is that should the rooks be exchanged, White's queenside majority could become dangerous. The natural 22 b3 ♘b6 23 ♗b2 (not 23 ♗d2? ♘e4! 24 ♘xe4 ♗xd4, winning material) 23...♘c4 24 ♗c1 ♘b6 25 ♗b2 results in a draw by repetition, which was sensible and congruent with the my assessment of this position.

22 ♖b1?   ♘e4!
23 ♘xe4 *(127)*

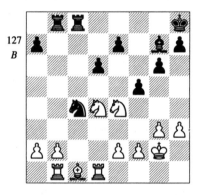

127
B

White doesn't sense the approaching danger. Vaganian thought a long time over his 22nd move. He now expected 23...fxe4 24 b3 with ♗g5 and ♘e6 to follow; in this variation White frees his position and even creates some pressure on Black's weaknesses. I rechecked my calculations and rubbed my eyes in disbelief when it was clear that the following tactic worked:

23 ...   ♘a3!!

My opponent was stunned, but didn't lose heart and began to examine carefully the various possibilities. After the game he claimed to have seen 23...♘a3, but: A) thought that it could not possibly work; B) assumed, on general grounds, that the resulting position, where he would have a strong central knight plus a pawn against Black's rook, would be at least equal for him.

It should be mentioned that the immediate 23...♗xd4 (intending to win by 24 ♖xd4 ♘a3 25 ♖a1 ♘c2) is not as strong, because of 24 b3!.

24 ♘xd6

Alternatives are:

a) 24 ♖a1? ♗xd4.

b) 24 ♘b3 ♘xb1 25 ♘g5 ♖c2!.

c) 24 ♘c3 ♘xb1 25 ♘xb1 ♗xd4.

d) 24 ♗e3 ♘xb1 25 ♘xd6 exd6 26 ♖xb1 ♖b4 27 ♘b3 ♖c2.

24 ...   exd6
25 ♗h6! *(128)*

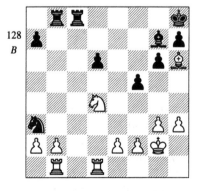

128
B

A counter-surprise that had escaped my attention. I now understood White's defensive plan, and realized that the ending would be difficult to win, especially against such a formidable opponent! But I believed there had to be a way to achieve victory, and indeed...

25	...	♘xb1
26	♗xg7+	♔xg7
27	♖xb1	♖c4! *(129)*

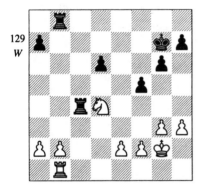

With this move, Black wins another pawn. Even then, laborious technical work is required to score the full point.

28	e3	♖a4
29	b3	

After 29 a3, 29...♖xa3 30 ♘c6! ♖b7 31 bxa3 gives White good drawing chances, but, according to the computer program Fritz3, Black can maintain winning chances by 29...♖b6 30 ♘c2 ♔f6.

29...♖xa2 30 ♖c1 a5! 31 g4 fxg4 32 hxg4 ♔f6 33 ♔g3 h5 34 ♖c6

♔e5 35 ♖c7 ♖h8! 36 gxh5 gxh5 37 ♖f7 ♔e4 38 ♖f4+ ♔d3

[The rest of the game is not relevant to our topic. Black won (0-1, 65).]

Discussion (by A.A.)

After two small surprises (8...♘c6, diverging from the usual 8...d6 and ...♘bd7; and 16...♘a5!, initiating a queen exchange), Black unleashed a major coup with 23...♘a3!!.

What I find remarkable in this ingenious tactical fracas, is both sides' calmness under fire. Neither Kogan's 23...♘a3!, nor Vaganian's 25 ♗h6! caused them to lose their coolness, or distorted their objectivity. Surprise is a potent weapon, but, as mentioned before, not overwhelming in itself. In this game, I feel that its effect was minimal. Rather, it was the intrinsic strength of the moves that decided the issue.

Ilan Manor – Rune Djurhuus
Groningen European Junior Ch 1986
Exchange Slav
Notes: GM Ilan Manor

1	d4	d5
2	c4	c6
3	cxd5	cxd5
4	♘f3	♘f6
5	♘c3	♘c6
6	♗f4	♗g4
7	♘e5	♕b6

8	♕d2!?	♕xd4
9	♕xd4	♘xd4 *(130)*

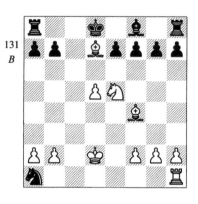

131
B

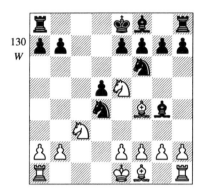

130
W

10 e4!!

My opponent expected an ordinary move such as 10 0-0-0, 10 ♖c1 or 10 ♖d1. The text-move, disregarding Black's forking threat, came as a surprise.

10	...	♘c2+?!
11	♔d2	♘xa1
12	♗b5+	♗d7
13	♘xd5!	♘xd5?!
14	♗xd7+	♔d8
15	exd5 *(131)*	
15	...	e6

It transpires that after 15...f6 16 ♗e6! fxe5 17 ♗xe5 Black is paralysed.

16	dxe6	♗b4+
17	♔e2	fxe6
18	♖xa1	♖f8
19	g3	♔e7
20	♖d1	♖f5
21	♗a4	g5
22	♖d7+	♔f8

23	♖xb7	gxf4
24	♘d7+	♔g8
25	♖xb4	1-0

I'm not sure if the play is analytically correct [**10...dxe4** (11 ♘b5 ♘e6; 11 ♘xg4 ♘xg4 12 ♘b5 e5; 11 f3 exf3 12 0-0-0 ♘c6) and **13...♗xb5** (14 ♘c7+ ♔d8 15 ♘xf7+ ♔d7 16 ♘xa8 g5!) are two possible improvements for Black]. Anyhow, my surprising tenth move achieved its aim.

Discussion (by A.A.)

The preceding game, Vaganian-Kogan, witnessed surprise in a minor role. Here, on the other hand, it plays the first violin. Manor adopts a practical approach: his 10 e4 may not be 100% sound, yet he relies on its unfamiliar and unexpected features to gain success.

His opponent is bewildered by the novel situation and fails to find the right path.

Ram Soffer – Mark Tseitlin
Israeli League 1993
Grünfeld Defence
Notes: GM Ram Soffer

[The bulk of the following commentary is taken, with permission, from the Israeli magazine *Schahmat*, where it was first published in 1993. At my request, GM Soffer kindly supplied additional notes, which appear in italics. (A.A.)].

Almost every chess player has, on occasion, fathered a theoretical novelty; to do that, it is sufficient to hit upon a move that does not appear in books or databases. Sometimes the move turns out to be superior to well-known 'theoretical' moves; sometimes not.

A new idea may be discovered during analysis of a topical opening variation. Alternatively, a novelty is found when a player is dissatisfied with the outcome of the opening in a certain game, and attempts to improve this variation in the comfort of his home laboratory.

Not all prepared innovations succeed. The factor of surprise and the work done before a game are supposed to give the innovator an edge, but other factors may work against him. During his home-analysis he may get carried away, become over-enthusiastic and overrate his chances, ignoring his opponent's resources.

At times, the resulting positions are so complicated that it is virtually impossible to arrive at an accurate conclusion without practical experience.

There is more: it can happen that a player fails to recall his prepared analysis. As a matter of fact, this has happened even to the current world champion, Garry Kasparov (on several occasions!). Even more frustrating is when a 'novelty' that took us many hours to conceive, turns out to be familiar to our opponent!

All these factors align in the following game.

1	d4	♘f6
2	c4	g6
3	♘c3	d5
4	♘f3	♗g7
5	♕b3	

At the time, this was my main line against the Grünfeld. Until the present game, I had never lost a tournament game with it.

5	...	dxc4
6	♕xc4	0-0
7	e4	a6

Black's most ambitious line. It is aimed at dislodging White's queen with ...b5, followed by ...c5: a temporary pawn sacrifice that gives Black an active game.

8	e5	b5
9	♕b3	♘g4
10	h3	

The variation 9...♘g4 was considered for many years to be one of

Black's strongest ripostes to the 5 ♕b3 variation. The cure was found a year later: 10 ♗d3! (with the idea 10...c5 11 ♗e4), which I used in several games in 1994. This move changed the theoretical evaluation of the variation. After Black's best continuation, 10...♗b7 11 h3 ♘h6 12 ♗xh6 ♗xh6 13 ♗e4, White obtains a small, yet solid advantage.

In retrospect, all the work I had invested in this variation in previous years was redundant; looking back, I can only marvel how I failed to detect 10 ♗d3 long ago.

10   ...   ♘h6

My first encounter with this position arose in a friendly five-minute game vs GM Kudrin in 1987. I remember that he sacrificed a pawn with ...c5, and after I accepted this sacrifice, he followed with ...♗e6, ...♘c6 ...♕a5 and my position quickly fell apart.

It took a lot of work to revive the variation. Against M. Hoffman, Bad Wörishofen 1991, I played 11 ♗f4 c5 12 ♕d5!? cxd4 13 ♕xa8 dxc3 14 b4 ♕c7 (½-½, 48). In search of a better move, 11 a4 seemed natural, but I didn't fancy 11...♘f5. Perhaps this knight should first be liquidated by 11 ♗xh6!?.

This move has some advantages: it prevents ...♘f5, deflects the black bishop from the long diagonal, gaining time to bring the rook to d1, if necessary. Admittedly, there are also

drawbacks: it relinquishes a bishop. After hours of analysis, I came to conclude that with correct play, White was assured of an edge in all variations. Therefore...

11   ♗xh6!?   ♗xh6
12   a4   c5

I expected my novelty to unsettle my opponent's tranquillity, but he proceeded confidently and quickly; it was White who soon found himself in time-trouble. After the game I found out, to my astonishment, that precisely this continuation had been played in the game Dydyshko-Ma. Tseitlin, St Petersburg 1992!! All I had done was to 'rediscover the wheel'.

13   dxc5

If 13 ♕d5 then 13...cxd4! 14 ♕xa8 dxc3 15 ♕xb8 cxb2 16 ♖b1 ♕a5+ and Black wins. 13 d5 ♕a5! is also unattractive.

13   ...   ♗e6 (132)

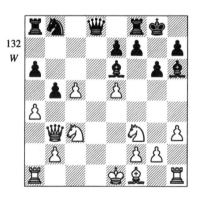

14   ♕b4!?

Here I made a basic error, deviating from my prepared line, 14 ♕a3, which is the only try for advantage.

It is difficult, three and a half years after the event, to reconstruct one's feelings during a game. Clearly, the fact that my opponent responded unhesitatingly, indicated that the position was not new to him. What happened during this game did not correspond to my experience in earlier games, in which I had employed prepared innovations. In those games my opponents deliberated a long time. It seems to me that Tseitlin's behaviour psychologically shook my confidence. I was afraid of a trap, did not rely upon my home-analysis (14 ♕a3) and wrongly deviated from it.

14	...	♘c6
15	♕h4	♔g7
16	♖d1	♕c7
17	axb5	axb5 (133)

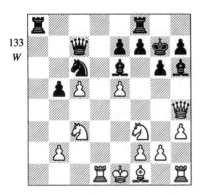

All this was played in the aforementioned game Dydyshko – Ma.

Tseitlin. Dydyshko chose 18 ♗xb5 and after 18...♘xe5 19 ♕d4 f6 20 ♘xe5 fxe5 Black's advantage was minute; the game ended in a draw. I was more concerned about 18...♗b3, but it transpires that after 19 ♖b1 ♗c2 20 0-0 ♗xb1 21 ♖xb1 White obtains counter-chances.

With my next move (played after long deliberation) I decided not to give up the exchange, but lost another tempo, enabling Black to initiate an attack on my uncastled king. Many compliments to my opponent for his superb play from now on.

18	♗d3?!	♗b3
19	♖b1	♖ad8!

The right rook. If now 20 ♕e4? f5! 21 exf6 e.p.+ exf6, the other rook occupies e8. 21 ♕e2 ♖xd3! 22 ♕xd3 ♗c4 is also unappetising.

20	♗xb5	♘xe5
21	♘d4	

The attack on the bishop generated some optimism, but that soon vanished after...

21	...	♗d2+!
22	♔e2 (134)	

22 ♔xd2 ♕xc5 23 ♔e3 f5 wins for Black. 22 ♔f1 is more stubborn, but even then Black maintains excellent chances.

22	...	♗a2!!

I must admit that this move was, to me, like a thunderbolt from a clear sky. If now 23 ♘xa2 ♕xc5 Black regains his material with a devastating attack, e.g. 24 b4 ♕b6 25 ♕e4 f6 26

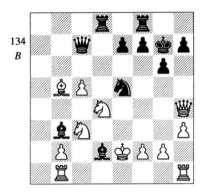

134
B

♘e6+ ♕xe6 27 ♖b2 f5. Nor will 23 ♖bd1 save the day, due to 23...♗xc3 24 bxc3 ♕xc5, with the double threat 25...♕xc3 and 25...♖xd4.

In time-trouble I selected an inferior defence:

23	♖a1?	♕xc5
24	♘a4	♗c4+
25	♔d1	♕xd4

...and after a few moves, **0-1**.

I don't recall thinking during the game that I had fallen into a self-spun net. It was only after 22...♗a2!! that I realized I was lost. Until that moment I believed in my chances.

After the game I concluded that against an adversary known for his sharp theoretical innovations, it is too risky to get involved in such variations. In my later encounters with Tseitlin, I adopted a saner approach to the opening, and was rewarded with several consecutive victories.

A painful defeat; still, it was interesting to be involved in this game, even on its losing end.

I hope that the fate of this 'novelty' will not deter readers from trying new ideas in their own games.

Discussion (by A.A.)

The game is a captivating illustration on the theme of 'the initiator gets caught in his own plot'. This is a *risk* inherent in every attempt to surprise one's opponent. We *think* it will come as surprise, but can never *know* for sure.

We certainly endorse Soffer's advice – to refrain from deducing from a single failure that innovative play in the opening is not profitable.

Tseitlin's reputation as a theoretician, plus this gloomy experience, generated in Soffer a *deterrence effect*: he will no longer engage this rival in a theoretical duel. This seems sensible: as the Latvian Gambit (1 e4 e5 2 ♘f3 f5) may be appropriate to employ against some opponents, so the weapon of surprise should be used against particular opponents, not as a universal weapon.

Instances where an apparently 'new' move has already been played and analysed, are common. The need to be familiar with recent publications is evident. Of course, human memory and the number of working hours at our disposal are not limitless. Playing a move that our opponent has encountered just recently is, perhaps, simply bad luck.

7 Summary

In the last quarter of the twentieth century, the body of chess knowledge has expanded enormously; the rate of spreading this knowledge took an accelerated pace; the ability of chess enthusiasts to digest and make sense of great chunks of data, having been enhanced by a host of sophisticated computerized tools.

All this has apparently made the task of the ambitious chess player somewhat easier. Emanuel Lasker declared, in his time, that he could elevate an ordinary man with no special gifts for chess to the level of a first-category player within a short period of time. It appears that in the present age, this 'ordinary man', provided he is earnest; a hard-worker, helped by a dedicated trainer, sponsored to compete in various tournaments and assisted by modern learning tools, can reach the rank of an IM within three or four years from having taken up competitive chess seriously.

Browsing through modern magazines, it is striking to notice that what was, until recently, accomplished by only a selected few, has become a common knowledge. Rubinstein's magic play in rook endings has been mastered presently by lesser mortals; Botvinnik's deep methods of opening preparation are implemented regularly by young aspirants; original ways of attack, found 40 years ago (for instance, knight or bishop sacrifices on d5, b5 or e6 in the Sicilian Defence) have become stock weapons of beginners.

Strangely, the fact that so many are able to attain a high level, creates a new problem. If *everybody* knows how to handle 'hanging pawns'; if the ending of ♖+♙ vs ♖ is perfectly assimilated by *all*; if the theory of the Slav is at the fingertips of *any* child; what, then, are the weapons left to decide the fate of chess battles?

As I see it, non-chessic weapons have become deciding factors. Players who possess advanced skills of withstanding pressure; with a superior acquaintance of deception techniques; who show a subtler grasp of psychological ploys; with an aptitude for 'learning how to learn', will dominate the field.

In a world where pure chess weapons are in the possession of a wide public, nuances in non-chess weapons can make the difference between success and failure.

Surprise is such a weapon.

It is a relatively little-explored and only partly understood phenomenon. An expert on surprise claims that:

"Even after nations find themselves on the receiving end of nasty surprises, they abstain from delving into the question *'why* were they caught by surprise'. Instead, they are satisfied with drawing some situational lessons (so as not to repeat similar mistakes)" (Lanir, 1989).

The more I became engrossed in this work, the more I realized how little we understand the phenomenon of a chess-context surprise. The following anecdote will illustrate my point:

At my request, a respected GM had sent me a game of his, that he valued as surprising. I returned him a phone-call: "Thank you for the lovely game" – I said – "can you please tell me *why* you find the play surprising?"

The GM was clearly annoyed: "Why, it looks surprising to me" – he said – "it is, well, unexpected ... my opponent thought so too ... Don't you agree?"

"Yes, I do" – I concurred – "but *why*? What causes the surprise?"

To this (stupid?) question, the GM had no answer.

To my mind, to say that an idea or a move is surprising because it is unexpected (or vice versa), is not very helpful. To infuse meaning into such a phrase, we have to unravel the tacit assumptions and expectations of the contestants. Only if we identify what

is *expected,* can surprise (the *unexpected*) be defined, planned and countered.

In the process of the present exploration of chess surprises, some interesting observations were made. We came to appreciate:

- the impact of surprise, disregarding the move/plan's objective merits
- the various forms surprise may take
- the viability of planning ahead a surprising operation, thus viewing 'surprise' not only in retrospect
- the distinction between risk-taking and sacrifice of material
- the role of multi-purpose moves
- advantages of a peculiar playing-style
- feasibility of surprise in situations where nothing, apparently, is happening (delayed action; surprise by habituation)
- benefits of psychological ploys
- identification of certain situations that are liable to catch most of us unaware
- coping with the enemy's schemes by imagining possible scenarios
- the vital function of good nerves in reacting to surprise
...and more.

Understanding underlying mechanisms of surprise (in chess and in other fields), its effect and the reasons behind it, is invaluable. Acquiring the capacity to plan and execute an unexpected operation that will subvert the game from its course is a more important skill than it has ever been before.

Bibliography

1. Z. Lanir / *Intelligence as a myth* / *Politics* 5/1989 (in Hebrew).

8 Assorted Surprises

In our final chapter, the reader is invited to see if he can spot the following selection of surprises.

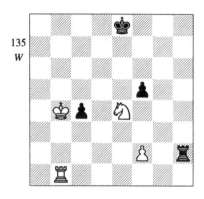

135
W

From a study by Alexander Sarychev, 3rd Prize, *Szachy*, 1972
White to play and win

White's task is two-fold: to bring his knight to safety and, at the same time, to conserve his only remaining pawn. Forming a battery along the d-file comes to mind: **1 ♘d6+ ♚d7?** **2 ♖d1 ♖xf2? 3 ♘e4+**; but what if Black improves with **1...♚e7!** instead?

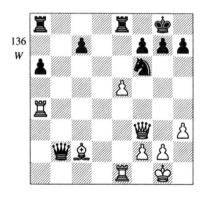

136
W

de Firmian – Benjamin
USA Ch 1988
White to play and win

Black has just captured a pawn on b2. The means that White employs to force victory are quite surprising.

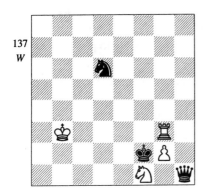

From a study by P. Arestov, 2nd Prize, *Shakhmaty Vestnik*, 1993
White to play and draw

Pursuing a difficult goal, one is supposed to play actively and vigorously. However, sometimes the solution takes a different course.

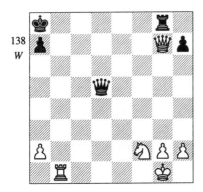

Ullrich – Spengler
Berlin 1948
White to play

The white queen cannot move on account of mate. Surprise tactics by *both* sides lead to an unexpected result.

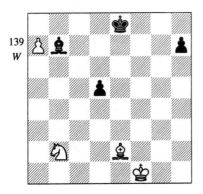

From a study by A. Maksimovskikh and V. Shupletsov, 2nd Commendation, *Magadan Komsomolets*, 1985
White to play and win

Black's plan, to capture the a-pawn, appears unanswerable: 1 ♘a4 ♔d8 2 ♘b6 only draws after 2...♔c7 3 a8♕ ♗xa8 4 ♘xa8+ ♔b7. Drastic measures are required.

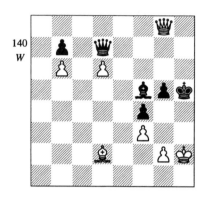

Uhlmann – Clarke
Hastings 1959
White to play

A remarkable idea to remove the blockading black queen starts with an absurd-looking move.

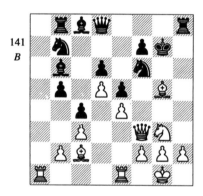

Hübner – Beliavsky
Munich 1990
Black to play

White has sacrificed a piece for two pawns and enduring pressure. Particularly annoying is the pin along the h4-d8 diagonal. Black's forthcoming plan is original and unexpected.

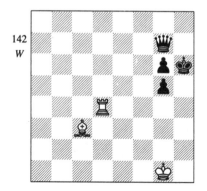

J. Kricheli, 1986
White to play and win

Do you remember our discussion about positions in which the enemy seems incapable of doing any harm? Here is a case in point. It looks improbable that White can *draw* with a rook and bishop vs queen + two pawns; can he possibly *win*?

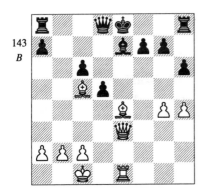

Hommeles – Skoblikov
Dutch team Ch 1992
Black to play

White has invested material in order to achieve an attacking position.
21...0-0? is not on due to 22 ♗xe7,
21...♗xc5? 22 ♕xc5 is too dangerous, and if 21...dxe4 22 ♕xe4, White
regains his material, e.g. 22...0-0 23
♗xe7 ♕a5 with equality. Uncon-
vinced by White's compensation,
Black went after the winning attempt
21...♔f8, expecting 22 ♗xd5 ♕xd5
23 ♕xe7+ ♔g8. What was the reply
to **21...♔f8**?

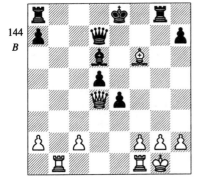

Dizdar – Chandler
Jurmala 1983
Black to play

Black played **1...♖xg2+ 2 ♔xg2
♕g4+ 3 ♔h1 ♕f3+** and a draw was
agreed. Doesn't **3...♕f4** win?

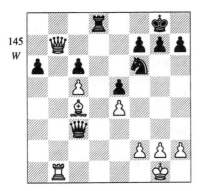

Krasenkov – Hickl
Jakarta 1996
White to play

White exerts strong pressure
against Black's weak f7-point; the
direct 23 ♕xf7+ suggests itself, but
after 23...♔h8 there is nothing decisive for White. However...

Solutions

135) **1 ♘d6+ ♚e7 2 ♘xf5+ ♚e6**

2...♚f6? 3 ♘g3 and White wins.

3 ♘d4+ ♚d5

Notice how, during the first three moves, the composer leads us to expect that the correct idea lies in creating a *vertical* battery, against the black *king*.

4 ♖b2!!

4 ♖d1? ♖xf2 draws; the text-move forms a *horizontal* battery, targeting the *rook*.

4...♚xd4 5 ♖d2+ ♚e4

Or 5...♚e5 6 f4+.

6 f3+

White wins.

136) **22 ♖e2! ♕b5**

He has to defend against 23 exf6 and 23 ♗xh7+. 22...♕c1+ 23 ♚h2 ♘d7 loses to 24 ♗xh7+ ♚xh7 25 ♕xf7.

23 ♖a1!

Fresh threats: 24 ♗a4 and 24 ♗d3.

23...♘d7 24 ♗a4 ♕a5

24...♘xe5 25 ♕xa8!.

25 e6! fxe6 26 ♖ee1!

Reuniting his rooks, White wins material and the game. It is not often that retreating moves like ♖a4-a1! and ♖e2-e1! are so powerful.

26...♕d5 27 ♕xd5 exd5 28 ♖xe8+ ♖xe8 29 ♗xd7 ♖d8 30 ♗c6 ♖d6 31 ♖xa6 1-0

137) **1 ♖h3! ♕g1**

White draws more easily after either 1...♕xf1? 2 ♖f3+ or 1...♕xg2? 2 ♖h2.

2 ♖c3!!

It transpires that Black cannot disentangle the royal couple.

2...♚e2 3 ♘g3+ ♚d2 4 ♖c2+ ♚e3

4...♚d1 5 ♖c1+! draws.

5 ♖c3+ ♚f2

Forced.

6 ♘f1!

Back to base.

6...♕h1 7 ♖h3 ♕g1 8 ♖c3! ♘e4 9 ♖c2+ ♚e1 10 ♖c1+ ♚f2

10...♚e2? 11 ♘g3+.

11 ♖c2+

With a draw.

138) **1 ♖b5!**

1 ♖d1?? ♕xd1+.

1...♖e8!

This threatens both 2...♖e1# and 2...♕xb5.

2 ♖b1!

Strangely, the only move.

2...♖g8

...and after **3 ♖b5!** it is a draw by repetition!

139) **1 ♗a6!!**

What a move! White wins in every line:

a) **1...♗a8 2 ♘a4 ♔d8 3 ♘b6.**

b) **1...♗xa6+ 2 ♘c4! ♗b7** (or 2...♗xc4+ 3 ♔ moves) **3 ♘d6+.**

c) **1...♗c6 2 ♘c4!! ♔d8** (2...dxc4 3 ♗b5!) **3 ♘a5 ♗a8 4 ♗b7.**

140) **1 g4+! fxg3+ e.p. 2 ♔g1!**

2 ♔xg3? ♕xd6+; or 2 ♔g2? ♗h3+ 3 ♔xg3 ♕xd6+ 4 ♔xh3 ♕d7+! with a draw.

2...♗g6

There was no other way to protect the vulnerable g5-pawn.

3 ♔g2! ♕f5

In the game Black chose 3...♔h6 4 ♕h8+ ♔h7 5 ♕f6+ ♔g6 6 ♕xg5+ and resigned (6...♔g7 7 ♗c3+).

4 ♕h8+ ♗h7 5 ♕d4! ♕d7 6 ♕g4+! ♕xg4 7 fxg4+

...and **8 d7**, winning.

141) **23...♔g6!!**

It turns out that the pin cannot be maintained: 24 h4 ♗g4! (formerly impossible, due to 25 ♗xf6 *check*!) 25 ♗xf6 ♕d7! traps White's queen.

24 ♘f5 ♔xg5!

Audacious and strong. Now after 25 h4+ ♖xh4 26 ♘xh4 ♔xh4, White is unable to exploit the black king's precarious situation: 27 ♕g3+ ♔h5 28 ♗d1+ ♗g4 and Black wins.

25 ♕g3+ ♘g4 26 h4+ ♔f6!

He is alert to a counter-surprise: 26...♔h5? 27 ♕xg4+!! ♔xg4 28 ♗d1+ ♔f4 29 g3#!

27 ♕xg4 ♕g8 28 ♕f3 ♗xf5

Black is winning.

29 ♕xf5+ ♔e7 30 ♕h3 ♕g6 31 g3 ♘c5 32 ♔f1 ♕f6 0-1

142) **1 ♖d3 ♕a7+**

This is forced, on account of the double threat 2 ♖h3# and 2 ♗xg7+.

2 ♗d4 ♕d7

Forced again.

3 ♗g7+! ♕xg7 4 ♖h3#

So simple, yet unexpected and curious.

143) As we demonstrated, some ideas are surprising only because they are rare. White showed the fallacy of Black's last move by a magnificent one-move shot, seldom seen in practical play:

22 ♗h7!!

A quiet, non-capturing move, leaving material *en prise*. Now 22...♗xc5 23 ♕xc5+, 22...♖xh7 23 ♗e7+, and 22...♗d6 23 ♕e8+! ♕xe8 24 ♗xd6+ are all hopeless.

22...♕d7 23 ♗xe7+ ♔e8 24 ♗f5 ♕b7 25 ♗b4+ ♔d8 26 ♗a5+ 1-0

144) After 1...♖xg2+ 2 ♔xg2 ♕g4+ 3 ♔h1 ♕f4 White succeeds, through a series of *zwischenzugs*, to extricate his monarch:

4 ♕a4+ ♔f8

4...♔f7 5 ♕d7+ ♔xf6 6 ♕h3.

5 ♗e5!! ♗xe5

Or 5...♕xe5 6 f4.

6 ♕a3+! ♔f7 7 ♕g3

Or 7 ♕h3. Hence, the result was justified.

145) The delayed action **23 ♕c7!!** proves deadly. Black's rook is short of a good square: 23...♖a8 24 ♖b8+; 23...♖e8 24 ♗xf7+; or 23...♖f8 24 ♕xf7+!. Amusingly, victory is gained by forcing Black to cover f7! The game continuation was **23...♕d4 24 ♗d5! 1-0**.

Index of Players and Composers

Numbers refer to pages. When it appears in **bold**, the player had the white pieces. Those in *italic* are for compositions.

Adams	**45**	Doda	83
Addison	76	Douven	69
Afek	**91**	Dzindzichashvili	31
Agdestein	74	Ettlinger	**78**
Alterman	80	Euwe	75
Anand	27, **30**	Feurstein	**47**
Andersson	44 (2), 45	Fischer	67
Andruet	61	Fishbein	**26**
Arestov	*105*	Flohr	**39**
Ashley	**47**	Fuchs	**48**
Avni	**60**, *60*	Gelfand	**15**
Baratz	36	Ghizdavu	**65**
Bareev	28	Grinberg	55
Beim	66	Grob	39
Beliavsky	107	Grooten	**30**
Benjamin	104	Grünfeld, Y.	66
Bennet	47	Gufeld	51
Bernstein, O.	**73**	Gurevich, M.	59
Bertok	**13**	Gurgenidze, D.	*55*
Boersma	**69**	Gusev	*64*
Botterill	**44**	Haines	51
Botvinnik	**67, 75**	Halliwell	29
Bouwmeester	**71**	Har-Zvi	91
Bryson	**61**	Hawes	**49**
Calvo	**76**	Hebden	58
Capablanca	78	Heller	**89**
Carmel	**66**	Hennigan	**59**
Chandler	108	Hertneck	**29**
Chapman	**29**	Hickl	109
Clarke	107	Høi	28
Colle	70	Hommeles	**109**
Czerniak	**13**	Honfi	48
Damjanović	13	Hübner	**107**
Davies	**79**	Hurme	77
de Firmian	**104**	Kagan	**49**
Deep Blue	**14**	Kasparov	14, **27**, 30, **44**, 51
Dembo	**50**	Kataev	76
Dizdar	**108**	Katalymov	37
Djurhuus	95	Kerr	49

Khalifman	71, 79
Khuzman	**41**, 42
Kogan	93
Korchnoi	**42**
Kosashvili	**90**
Krasenkov	**109**
Krays	**76**
Kricheli	*108*
Kudrin	42
Kuznetsov, An.	*64*
Lalić, B.	**28**
Larsen	**28**
Lengyel	86
Leonhardt	**68**
Lilienthal	32
Liss	**86**
Lutz	36
Mabbs	**49**
Makarychev	**52**
Maksimovskikh	*106*
Mannheimer	48
Manor	**95**
Matulović	**34, 77**
Mieses	68
Mikhalchishin	**11**
Miles	30
Mohrlok	49
Mukhin	**37**
Murey	**55**
Najdorf	77, 105
Naumkin	52
NN	**48**
Ortega	34
Pachman	**83**
Perenyi	**63**
Petkevich	68
Pinter	**80**
Pirc	71
Plaskett	**14, 58**
Pletanek	79
Polgar, J.	29
Polugaevsky	**51**
Porper	60
Portisch	63
Pritchett	32
Rabar	**105**

Ragozin	**32**
Ratner	50
Rechlis	89, 90
Reshevsky	**63**
Richi	13
Richter, K.	**36**
Ristoja	32
Root	26
Sakharov	31
Sarychev	*104*
Seirawan	63 (2)
Shabalov	47
Sher	61
Shigapov	*62*
Shirov	15, **36, 74**
Shmuter	49
Shupletsov	*106*
Skoblikov	109
Soffer	**97**
Soto Larrea	**34**
Spassky	**63**
Speelman	14
Spengler	106
Steniczka	*7, 8 (2), 8, 9*
Stoltz	**70**
Sutovsky	**42, 66**
Timman	65, **71**
Tompa	**61**
Tseitlin, Ma.	97
Tsvetkov	34
Uhlmann	**107**
Ullrich	**106**
Unzicker	77
Vaganian	**93**
Varga	34
Vidmar	73
Vlasak	*79*
Wapner	**34**
Westerinen	11
Winants	**51**
Wotawa	*12*
Yandarbiev	**38**
Yosha	**51**
Yurtaev	41
Zagalov	38
Zhukhovitsky	**68**